Butterworths Student Companion

CONSTITUTIONAL

Butterworths Student Companion

CONSTITUTIONAL

**Case Digests
Prepared by Bruce Petrie**

Butterworths

Toronto and Vancouver

Butterworths Student Companion: Constitutional

The Butterworth Group of Companies

Canada:
Butterworths Canada Ltd.,
75 Clegg Road, MARKHAM, Ontario L6G 1A1
and
1721-808 Nelson St., Box 12148, VANCOUVER, B.C. V6Z 2H2

Australia:
Butterworths Pty Ltd., SYDNEY, ADELAIDE, BRISBANE, CANBERRA, HOBART, MELBOURNE and PERTH

Ireland:
Butterworth (Ireland) Ltd., DUBLIN

Malaysia:
Malayan Law Journal Sdn Bhd, KUALA LUMPUR

New Zealand:
Butterworths of New Zealand Ltd., WELLINGTON and AUCKLAND

Puerto Rico:
Butterworths of Puerto Rico, Inc., SAN JUAN

Singapore:
Butterworths Asia, SINGAPORE

South Africa:
Butterworth Publishers (Pty.) Ltd., DURBAN

United Kingdom:
Butterworth & Co. (Publishers) Ltd., LONDON and EDINBURGH

United States:
Michie Butterworth, CHARLOTTESVILLE, Virginia

Canadian Cataloguing in Publication Data

Petrie, Bruce (Bruce D.)
Constitutional
(Butterworths student companions)
Includes index.
ISBN 0-433-39667-9

1. Canada - Constitutional law - Digests.
I. Title.   II. Series.
KE4216.9.P47 1995   342.71'002648   C95-932402-X
KF4482.P47 1995

Printed and bound in Canada.

PREFACE

One of the primary objectives for you as a law student is to learn to read cases in order to extract legal principles. Moreover, you must be able to understand each principle in the context of cases that have gone before, as well as how to apply it to fact situations in cases that will come after. And the process doesn't end in law school: as the law constantly evolves, new developments present a never ending task.

This Butterworths Student Companion is intended as an easy first reference in developing analytical skills, and also as a quick refresher once the cases have been fully studied and understood. You should not consider it a substitute for reading course materials, but rather as a handy study aid.

Leading cases have been organized according to subject, as found in a typical case book. Each digest summarizes the relevant facts, ratio and holding in a clear and straightforward manner; extraneous facts, obiter, and ratio unrelated to the particular topic are omitted. This selection of cases does not attempt to be the last word on the area of constitutional law; you should also refer to a casebook such as Whyte, Lederman & Bur's *Canadian Constitutional Law*, 3rd edition, for more comprehensive coverage and for a fuller explanation of the development of each principle.

Learning to analyze cases is a long but rewarding journey. Bon voyage!

TABLE OF CONTENTS

TABLE OF CASES

(references are to digest number)

A

F

G

H

I

J

L

M

N

O

P

Q

R

S

T

U

V

W

Z

FEDERALISM

The Rule of Law

1. *In Re the Initiative and Referendum Act*
    [1919] A.C. 935 (P.C.)

The Legislative Assembly of Manitoba enacted the Initiative and Referendum Act. The statute allowed provincial laws to be made and repealed by direct vote of the electors of the province, in addition to those laws made and repealed by the Legislative Assembly. A certain proportion of the electorate could propose a new law by submitting a petition to the Legislative Assembly. The new law could then either be passed by the Assembly, submitted to a vote at the next general provincial election, or submitted to a referendum vote within six months of presentation of the petition. If the law was approved by a majority of the electors, it was to take effect as though it were a law passed by the Legislative Assembly.

A provincial Order-in-Council referred to the Court of King's Bench the question of whether the law was *intra vires* of the Provincial Legislature. An affirmative answer by the Court was reversed by the Manitoba Court of Appeal.

The Privy Council observed that under s. 92 of the British North America Act, each province was allowed to make laws amending its own constitution, with one exception being that a province could not make laws affecting the office of Lieutenant-Governor. However, the proposed law was construed as affecting the position of the Lieutenant-Governor as constitutional head of the Legislative Assembly. The Act would have the effect of excluding the Lieutenant-Governor from any legislative authority, contrary to the rights integral to that position. The Act was therefore held to be *ultra vires*.

2. *Roncarelli v. Duplessis*
    [1959] S.C.R. 121, 16 D.L.R. (2d) 689

The plaintiff, R, owned a restaurant which was licensed for the sale of alcoholic beverages. The defendant, D, was the Premier and Attorney General of the Province of Quebec. D authorized the cancellation of R's liquor licence. R brought an action for damages resulting from the cancellation of the licence. The action succeeded at trial but the decision was reversed on appeal.

R was a member of the Witnesses of Jehovah, a religious group whose members had been frequently charged with contravening City of Montreal by-laws respecting the distribution of printed material. Although R was never charged under these by-laws, he provided bail for many of those who were charged. It was accepted by a majority of the Supreme Court of Canada that D authorized the revocation of the liquor licence for no other reason than R's association with the Jehovah's Witnesses and his role in providing bail.

Under the Alcoholic Liquor Act, the Quebec Liquor Commission (the "Commission") was an independent body that could revoke licences at its discretion. However, the Court held that the discretion had to be exercised by weighing considerations which were pertinent to the administration of the Act. In this case, the licence was revoked to punish R for activities wholly unrelated to the purpose of the Act. In addition, it was found that the Commission would not have cancelled the licence without the order and authorization of D. D, as Attorney General, had no power to intervene in the administration of the Commission's affairs. It was observed that every public official is as responsible as any private citizen for any act done without legal justification. Since D was acting without authority he was liable under the Civil Code of Procedure for damages sustained by R.

Although art. 88 of the Civil Code provided that no public officer could be sued for damages for "any act done by him in the exercise of his functions" without proper notice, D's defence on this ground failed because it was held that he was acting wholly outside his legal functions. To deny R recovery for D's arbitrary, unauthorized actions would signal "the beginning of disintegration of the rule of law as a fundamental postulate of our constitutional structure" (J. D. Whyte, W. R. Lederman & D. F. Bur, *Canadian Constitutional Law: Cases, Notes and Materials*, 3rd ed., (Toronto: Butterworths, 1992) p. 1-16).

3.   *Reference re Language Rights Under the Manitoba Act, 1870*
[1985] 1 S.C.R. 72, 19 D.L.R. (4th) 1

Section 23 of the Manitoba Act, 1870, required that all statutes of the Province of Manitoba be published in both English and French. In 1890 the Legislative Assembly passed the Official Language Act which made English the official language of the courts and the Legislature. In 1985 the Governor-in-Council referred a question to the Supreme Court of Canada asking whether the language rights under s. 23 of the Manitoba Act, 1870 were mandatory and if so, whether the laws passed by the Provincial Legislature that had been printed and published in English only were invalid.

The Court answered both questions in the affirmative. The Court observed that under the rule of law, both government officials and private individuals are subject to the supremacy of the law. For that reason, the Court was required to follow the law as set out in s. 23 of the Manitoba Act, 1870, and s. 52 of the Constitution Act, 1982, to hold the unconstitutional laws of Manitoba to be of no force and effect. A second effect of the rule of law required the creation and maintenance of a set of positive laws to maintain law and order.

Thus, application of the rule of law required a declaration that the laws of the province were invalid. However, to declare the laws of the province invalid would destroy the legal order of the province and thus violate the rule of law. The Court recognized as a partial solution the *de facto* doctrine, imparting validity to official acts of persons who hold office under colour of authority. The Court similarly considered *res judicata* and mistake of law as potential relief from the consequences of the constitutional invalidity of the Manitoba statutes.

However, as these doctrines were seen to provide only limited assistance, the Court also relied on the doctrine of necessity. In order to uphold the rule of law, the Court declared that the rights and obligations arising under the invalid laws would have the same force and effect they would have had if they had arisen under constitutionally valid enactments. Such declared validity would last only until such time as the province was able to translate, re-enact, print and publish its Acts in both English and French.

Historical Development of Canadian Constitutional Law

4. *British Coal Corporation v. The King*
   [1935] A.C. 500 (P.C.)

The appellant, B, and four other companies had been convicted in the Quebec Court of King's Bench (Crown Side) of offences under the Combines Investigation Act. The conviction was upheld by the Court of King's Bench (Appeal Side) and B petitioned for leave to appeal to the Privy Council. There was a preliminary objection to the validity of the petition on the basis of s. 17 of an Act to amend the Criminal Code [referred to as "Canadian Statute"]. That section provided that no criminal appeals would be brought from a Canadian court to a court of the United Kingdom.

In ruling on the objection, the Privy Council reviewed the nature of appeals from Canadian courts. The Judicial Committee of the Privy Council was established to hear appeals from dominion and colonial courts. Subsequent legislation authorized Her Majesty in Council to override any colonial laws limiting or excluding such appeals. The issue arose in the Canadian context in the case of *Nadan v. The King*, [1926] A.C. 482, which concerned a provision of the Canadian Criminal Code that purported to restrict leave to appeal of criminal matters to Canadian courts. The Privy Council held the provision to be invalid as being repugnant to the Colonial Laws Validity Act, 1865. However, that case had been decided before the passage of the Statute of Westminster, 1931, which curtailed the application of the Colonial Laws Validity Act.

The Privy Council thus observed, in the present case, that in interpreting the British North America Act (the "BNA Act"), the "construction most beneficial to the widest possible amplitude of its powers must be adopted" (at 518 A.C.). Thus, without the *Nadan* case as a precedent, the Court observed that, in order to limit royal prerogative, a statute must deal with the prerogative by express terms or necessary intendment, and the statute must be endowed with the requisite power by an Imperial Act. It was held that s. 17 precisely stated a restriction on the royal prerogative, and that s. 91 of the BNA Act invested the Dominion Parliament with the power to legislate such a restriction. The petition was therefore dismissed with no decision on the merits.

5. *Attorney General for Ontario v. Attorney General for Canada (Privy Council Appeals Case)*
   [1947] A.C. 127 (P.C.)

In 1939 the Canadian Parliament introduced a bill which provided for the Supreme Court of Canada to be the final court of appeal in all civil and criminal matters within and for Canada. Under the bill, notwithstanding any royal prerogative or anything contained in any statute of the United Kingdom or Canada, no appeals would lie from a Canadian court to the Judicial Committee of the Privy Council. The Governor General-in-Council referred to the Supreme Court of Canada the question of whether enactment of the bill was *intra vires* of the Parliament of Canada. The Supreme Court upheld Parliament's competence to enact the bill.

The Attorneys General for Ontario, British Columbia and New Brunswick appealed the decision, alleging that the subject matter of the bill fell within the exclusive powers of the provincial legislatures. The Attorneys General for Canada, Manitoba and Saskatchewan, as respondents in the appeal, contended that the bill was *intra vires* under s. 101 of the British North America Act ("BNA Act"), or alternatively under s. 92.

The Privy Council observed that under the authority of s. 101 of the BNA Act the Parliament of Canada had passed the Supreme Court of Canada Act in 1875. This Act provided for appeals beyond the Supreme Court only under the exercise of royal prerogative. In 1931, the Imperial Parliament passed the Statute of Westminster, allowing Commonwealth Dominions to repeal or amend any Act of Parliament of the United Kingdom in so far as any such Act was part of the law of the Dominion. Against this historical background the Privy Council considered the question under two heads: appeals from the Supreme Court of Canada and appeals directly from provincial courts.

On appeals from the Supreme Court of Canada, the Privy Council held that the power of the Dominion Parliament to establish the Supreme Court was originally restricted by royal prerogative, but the restriction was subsequently removed by the Statute of Westminster. That portion of the legislation was thus held to be *intra vires*.

Regarding appeals from the provinces, the Privy Council held that s. 101 of the BNA Act provided the Parliament of Canada with the power to legislate in regard to appellate jurisdiction. Their Lordships observed that it is "a prime element in the self-government of the Dominion, that it should be able to secure through its own courts of justice that the law should be one and the same for all its citizens" (at 154 S.C.R.). The only way to ensure that result would be to allow s. 101 to authorize a court of both final and exclusive appellate jurisdiction. The appeal was dismissed.

6. *Reference re Amendment of the Constitution of Canada*
[1981] 1 S.C.R. 753, 125 D.L.R. (3d) 1

The Canadian House of Commons and Senate adopted a resolution presenting to Her Majesty the Queen in right of the United Kingdom a request to patriate the British North America Act, 1867. The name of the Act would be changed to the Constitution Act and would include a new amending procedure as well as a Charter of Rights and Freedoms. No Acts passed by the Parliament of the United Kingdom would extend to Canadian law after patriation. Ontario and New Brunswick were the only two provinces to approve the resolution.

On behalf of the remaining provinces, constitutional questions were referred to the Courts of Appeal of Manitoba, Newfoundland and Quebec. The decisions of these three courts were appealed to the Supreme Court of Canada.

The Manitoba reference asked three questions: (1) Would enactment of the resolution affect federal-provincial relationships, and if so, to what effect? (2) Is it a constitutional convention that such a resolution would not be presented to the Parliament of the United Kingdom without first obtaining the agreement of the provinces? (3) Is the agreement of the provinces constitutionally required for the proposed amendments contained in the Resolution?

The Newfoundland reference asked the same three questions and added a fourth: could the Terms of Union or s. 3 of the British North America Act, 1871, be amended without the consent of the Government of Newfoundland?

The Quebec Reference asked whether enactment of the proposed amendments would affect the legislative competence or the status of the provincial legislatures in virtue of the Constitution, and whether the Constitution empowers the Senate and House of Commons to amend the Constitution without the consent of the provinces and in spite of the objection of several of them.

The first question in the Manitoba reference was answered in the affirmative by all members of the Supreme Court. The proposed Charter of Rights and Freedoms would limit the powers of the provincial legislatures. The second question was answered by a majority of the Court in the affirmative. To determine whether a convention exists it is necessary to look at the precedents, to determine whether the actors in the precedents believed they were bound by a rule, and to assess whether or not there is a reason for the rule. There was a convention which required a measure of provincial agreement, though not unanimous provincial agreement. A majority of the Court answered the third question in the negative, rejecting an argument that a convention has or may crystallize into a rule of law.

The fourth question from the Newfoundland reference was largely adopted from the decision of the Newfoundland Court of Appeal, which indicated that the proposed resolution would not allow the changes to be made without the consent of the Newfoundland Legislative Assembly, but that the amending formula in the proposed Constitution Act could change the situation.

The first question from the Quebec reference was answered in the affirmative, for the same reasons given in the first question to the Manitoba reference. Regarding the second Quebec question, a majority of the Court answered in the negative as a matter of convention, but in the affirmative as a matter of law.

Constitutional Interpretation

7. *Citizens Insurance Company v. Parsons*
    (1881), 7 App. Cas. 96 (P.C.)

The Province of Ontario enacted legislation which provided for a set of statutory conditions deemed to be contained in every fire insurance policy in the province. The respondent, P, took out a fire insurance policy with the appellant, C. P made a claim on his policy which was denied by C on the grounds that P had failed to disclose pertinent information contrary to the conditions of the policy. P alleged that the conditions did not comply with the provincial insurance legislation. C argued that the legislation was *ultra vires*. P's action to recover under the policy succeeded at trial, and appeals to the Court of Appeal and the Supreme Court of Canada were dismissed.

The Privy Council observed that there is by necessity some overlap between the classes of subjects over which the Dominion Parliament and provincial legislatures have authority, as enumerated in s. 91 and s. 92, respectively, of the British North America Act. In situations of overlap, the courts are to ascertain and define the limits of the federal and provincial power. In cases of conflict, courts are required to read the two sections together to allow the language of one to interpret and modify that of the other, "without entering more largely upon an interpretation of the statute than is necessary for the decision of the particular question in hand" (Whyte, Lederman & Bur, p.4-34).

Using this approach, the Privy Council assessed whether or not the impeached legislation fell within any of the classes of subjects enumerated in s. 92. P alleged that it concerned "property and civil rights in the province". The Court agreed, rejecting C's argument for a narrow interpretation of "civil rights". With respect to the classes of subject enumerated in s. 91, only "the regulation of trade and commerce" was advanced in argument. The Court held that the authority of the Dominion Parliament to legislate for the regulation of trade and commerce did not include the power to regulate the contracts of a particular business or trade. Therefore, there was no conflict between federal and provincial legislative authority, and the Ontario legislation was valid.

8.   *Hodge v. The Queen*
        (1883), 9 App. Cas. 117 (P.C.)

The appellant H was convicted before the police magistrate of allowing a game of billiards in his tavern in contravention of his liquor licence. The licence had been issued under the provincial Liquor License Act by the License Commissioners for the City of Toronto. The conviction was quashed by the Court of Queen's Bench for Ontario but restored by the Court of Appeal. The Court of Appeal held that the Ontario Legislature had no authority to enact legislation regarding the regulation of licensed houses. Further, even if the Legislature had such authority, it could not delegate it to the Board of Commissioners.

On further appeal, the Privy Council chose not to lay down any general rules for the construction of the British North America Act. The subject matter of the Liquor License Act was considered to be the regulation of the sale of liquor within a municipality, thus affecting matters of a local nature. There was no interference with the Dominion Parliament's power of regulation of trade and commerce, therefore the legislation was valid.

The argument that the Legislature had no authority to delegate its powers to the License Commissioners was seen as a misconception of the true character of provincial legislatures. In exercising its s. 92 powers, a provincial legislature does not act as a delegate, but acts with the same type of authority as that of the Dominion Parliament or the Imperial Parliament.

9.   *Tennant v. Union Bank of Canada*
        [1894] A.C. 31 (P.C.)

The plaintiff, T, was the assignee of an insolvent firm which was a debtor of the defendant, U. The sums advanced to the firm by U were secured by warehouse receipts. After the firm became insolvent U removed a quantity of lumber from the firm's premises. T brought an action against U for damages for conversion of the lumber. The action was dismissed at trial and on appeal.

On further appeal, the Privy Council held that the transactions were governed by s. 54 of the Bank Act, and therefore the warehouse receipts held by U constituted valid security. T alleged that the section was *ultra vires* the Dominion Parliament. The Privy Council observed that T's objection to the legislation could be upheld if it could be shown that the British North America Act absolutely debarred the Dominion Parliament from encroaching on s. 92 matters. However, s. 91 declared the paramount authority of the Dominion Parliament "notwithstanding anything in this Act." If Dominion legislation fell under any of the enumerated classes of subjects in s. 91, it would be valid even though it may incidentally affect property and civil rights in the province. Such was the case here. The taking of security by warehouse receipts in the course of the business of banking was a matter within the subject of banking as contemplated by s. 91. The section of the Bank Act was therefore valid and the appeal was dismissed.

10. *Union Colliery Company v. Bryden*
     [1899] A.C. 580 (P.C.)

Section 4 of the British Columbia Coal Mines Regulation Act provided that "no boy under the age of twelve years, and no woman or girl of any age, and no Chinaman, shall be employed . . . in any mine . . . below ground." The appellant, U, employed Chinese workers. The respondent, B, was a shareholder of U. B brought an action for a declaration that the company had no right to hire Chinese employees, and for an injunction restraining the company from hiring Chinese employees. B alleged that the Chinese workers posed a source of danger and injury. U denied the risk of injury and further alleged that s. 4 was *ultra vires* the Provincial Legislature. The declaration and injunction were granted at trial, and the decision was upheld on appeal.

The Privy Council held that the issue of whether or not the legislation was reasonable was irrelevant to the decision. The case was decided on the construction of the British North America Act. If s. 92 of the Act had stood alone, the legislation would have been valid as relating to "Property and Civil Rights in the Province". However, s. 91 extended to the Dominion Parliament the authority to legislate with respect to "naturalization and aliens". The pith and substance of s. 4 affected the employment of aliens or naturalized subjects. The section as it related to Chinese employees was therefore *ultra vires* the Provincial Legislature, and the appeal was allowed.

11. *Grand Trunk Railway v. Attorney General of Canada*
     [1907] A.C. 65 (P.C.)

The Dominion Parliament enacted legislation which prohibited railway companies from "contracting out" liability to pay damages for personal injury to their servants. The appellant, G, alleged that the legislation was *ultra vires* as being legislation in respect of civil rights. The respondent, A, contended that the legislation was truly railway legislation.

The Privy Council observed that provincial and Dominion legislation could overlap and both would be valid if the field is clear. If the field is not clear, the Dominion legislation would prevail. As such, although the legislation did affect civil rights, nothing turned on that point. The question was whether the law was truly ancillary to railway legislation. G argued that the legislation would have a far-reaching effect on the operation of the railway, and the Privy Council used this argument to conclude that the law was ancillary to railway legislation. The law was held to be *intra vires*, and G's appeal was dismissed.

12. *John Deere Plow Company v. Wharton*
     [1915] A.C. 330 (P.C.)

The appellant, J, was incorporated under the federal Companies Act and carried on business across Canada. The respondent, W, brought an action to restrain J from carrying on business in British Columbia. Under the British Columbia Companies Act, an extraprovincial company was required to be registered or licensed to carry on business in the province. A licence was refused to J because another company with the same name had already registered in the province. W's action was upheld by the British Columbia Supreme Court.

The Privy Council considered whether the Provincial legislation concerned "civil rights in the Province." The Court observed that an abstract logical definition of the scope of the words "civil rights" would be both impracticable and a possible source of embarrassment and injustice in future cases. If the phrase were interpreted literally it would encompass many of the other heads listed in s. 92 of the British North America Act and much of the field of s. 91. The Court therefore refrained from providing exhaustive definitions of the expressions set out in ss. 91 and 92 and chose to confine its decision to the issues before it.

"Civil rights in the Province", despite the generality of the phrase, could not apply in this situation where a more specific subject matter was enumerated, that being the incorporation of companies with provincial objects. However, the objects of J were not strictly provincial. As such, since the matter did not come within the class of subjects assigned exclusively to the provincial legislatures, jurisdiction belonged exclusively to the Dominion Parliament. Because it was decided that the province could not legislate so as to deprive a Dominion company of its status and powers, the relevant provisions of the British Columbia Companies Act were deemed inoperative.

13. *Attorney General for Ontario v. Reciprocal Insurers*
     [1924] A.C. 328, [1924] 1 D.L.R. 789 (P.C.)

In *Attorney General for Canada v. Attorney General for Alberta*, [1916] 1 A.C. 588, the Insurance Act of 1910 was pronounced *ultra vires* the Dominion Parliament. That statute created penalties for breach of licensing provisions, which was held to be an interference with the exercise of civil rights in the provinces. The Insurance Act of 1917 contained similar licensing provisions, but nothing in the Act made it compulsory for any association or firm or individual to obtain a licence as a condition of lawfully carrying on the business of insurance. However, an amendment to the Criminal Code made it an indictable offence to carry on the business of insurance without being duly licensed by the Minister of Finance.

A question as to the validity of the Criminal Code amendment was referred to the Supreme Court of Ontario, then to the Privy Council. The Dominion as Intervenor conceded that the true character of the legislation was the regulation of the exercise of civil rights, but argued that the criminal law jurisdiction of Parliament is unlimited.

The Privy Council construed the language of s. 91 in the context of s. 92 to reject that argument. Parliament could not appropriate for itself a field of jurisdiction belonging to the provinces simply by purporting to use s. 91 to create penal sanctions. The Criminal Code amendment was thus held to be invalid.

14. *Edwards v. Attorney General for Canada*
[1930] A.C. 124 (P.C.)

Section 24 of the British North America Act (the "BNA Act") provided for the appointment of "qualified persons" to the Senate. A group of five women petitioned for a reference to the Supreme Court of Canada asking whether the word "persons" included female persons.

The Supreme Court asserted that its role in answering the question was to interpret the provisions of the Constitution without considering any political aspects of the question. The Court observed that, at the time of Confederation, women were not allowed to hold public office. Therefore, at the time the BNA Act was framed they were not "qualified persons", and since that time the Imperial Parliament had done nothing to alter that fact. As such, the Supreme Court held that women were not eligible for appointment to the Senate.

The Privy Council allowed the appeal. Their Lordships stated that the BNA Act had "planted in Canada a living tree capable of growth and expansion within its natural limits" (Whyte, Lederman & Bur, p. 4-5). Provisions of the Act were not to be cut down by narrow and technical construction, but were to be given a large and liberal interpretation. Other sections of the Act expressly referred to male persons, but s. 24 did not. Section 24 referred to "qualified persons" and the word "qualified" was held to refer to s. 23, which set out the qualifications of a senator, none of which required that a senator be male. Therefore, it was held that women were eligible to become members of the Senate.

15.   *Provincial Secretary of P.E.I. v. Egan*
[1941] S.C.R. 396, [1941] 3 D.L.R. 305

The respondent, E, had been convicted under the Criminal Code of driving while intoxicated. As a result, his driver's licence was cancelled for 12 months under s. 84 of the P.E.I. Highway Traffic Act. About six months after the conviction, E applied for an operator's licence which was refused by the appellant P because the cancellation period had not yet expired. E appealed the decision to the County Court.

The County Court Judge allowed the appeal and ordered the Department of the Provincial Secretary to issue a licence. P appealed to the Supreme Court of P.E.I. on the grounds that the County Court Judge had no jurisdiction to make the order, and P had a right to refuse to issue the licence. The appeal was dismissed and a further appeal was taken to the Supreme Court of Canada.

The Supreme Court observed that in s. 8 of the Highway Traffic Act there was a right of appeal where there was a revocation of or refusal to grant a licence "under this section". In this case the suspension was under s. 84 and not under s. 8. Therefore there was no right of appeal and the Supreme Court of the province should have allowed the appeal and set aside the decision of the County Court Judge.

The Court went on to consider the constitutionality of s. 84 of the Highway Traffic Act in light of s. 285 of the Criminal Code. The former section provided for an automatic suspension of a driver's licence for 12 months for driving while intoxicated, while the latter section stated that a conviction would result in a prohibition from driving for a period not exceeding three years. It was held that the field of the two enactments was not co-extensive and both provisions could validly subsist together. The provincial statute dealt purely with civil rights in the province and did not add to or vary the punishment set out in the Criminal Code.

16.   *Attorney General for Saskatchewan v. Attorney General for Canada (Saskatchewan Farm Security Act)*
[1949] A.C. 110 (P.C.)

Section 6 of the Farm Security Act of Saskatchewan provided for adjustments to terms of payment of loans in the event of crop failure. It included a provision for a reduction in the payment of principal, but the amount of interest payable continued as though the principal had not been reduced. The respondent, AGC, contended that the provision was an enactment in relation to interest and thus *ultra vires* the provincial Legislature. The appellant, AGS, alleged that "agriculture in the Province" and "property and civil rights" formed the "pith and substance" of the section, and that it affected interest only incidentally (Whyte, Lederman & Bur, p. 4-43). The Supreme Court of Canada held that the enactment was *ultra vires* the Province.

On appeal, the Privy Council looked to the "true nature and character" of the legislation to interpret its provisions. The legislation related to contracts between farmers and moneylenders, and such legislation was construed not to be in relation to agriculture. On consideration of the substance of the enactment rather than at its form, the Privy Council concluded that this was legislation in relation to interest. Reducing the amount of principal while keeping the amount of interest constant had the effect of increasing the rate of interest. Because the legislation affected interest rates, it conflicted with provisions of the federal Interest Act. Therefore the legislation was held to be invalid as the provincial Legislature was attempting to do indirectly what it could not do directly. The provision could not be saved as being merely incidental to the topic of interest, because the Privy Council viewed interest as being "at the heart of the matter" (Whyte, Lederman & Bur, p. 4-45).

17. *Johnson v. Attorney General of Alberta*
[1954] S.C.R. 127, [1954] 2 D.L.R. 625

The Alberta Slot Machine Act provided that if a peace officer had reasonable and probable grounds to believe that a slot machine was being kept in a premises, the peace officer could swear an information before a justice of the peace to allow entry and search of the premises. Any slot machine discovered by the search would be seized, and the person in possession of the slot machine would have to appear before a justice to show cause why the seized machine should not be confiscated.

Several machines had been seized from the appellant, J, who had been notified to appear to show cause. The Supreme Court of Alberta granted an order prohibiting any further steps in the proceedings. The order was set aside by the Appellate Division, and J appealed to the Supreme Court of Canada on the question of whether the Slot Machine Act was *intra vires* the Provincial Legislature.

The Court interpreted the main object of the Act to be the prevention of gambling by forbidding the keeping of gambling machines. However, the Criminal Code had already made it an offence to buy, sell, keep or employ any gambling device, and had provided the means by which such devices could be seized and confiscated. Therefore, as the Criminal Code had already dealt with the subject matter of the Slot Machine Act, the provincial legislation simply duplicated the sanctions of the Code andinterfered with its administration. Furthermore, because the subject matter of the provincial statute could not be related to any of the heads listed in s. 92 of the British North America Act, the legislation was declared to be *ultra vires*. The appeal was allowed.

18. *McKay v. The Queen*
[1965] S.C.R. 798, 53 D.L.R. (2d) 532

The appellant, M, had been convicted by a justice of the peace of contravening a zoning by-law of the Township of Etobicoke. The by-law prevented the display of signs on residential premises, with certain limited exceptions. The exceptions did not specifically mention election signs. M was charged as a result of displaying a sign in support of a candidate who was running in the 1962 federal election. The conviction was quashed by a judge but was restored by the Ontario Court of Appeal. An appeal was taken to the Supreme Court of Canada, with M alleging that a true construction of the by-law did not forbid the conduct which was held to be an offence.

A majority of the Supreme Court held that to construe the by-law as was done by the justice of the peace and the Court of Appeal would destroy M's right to engage in a form of political activity in the federal field. The prohibition in the by-law was a law in relation to proceedings at a federal election and not in relation to any subject matter within provincial power. The by-law attempted to use general words to effect a result which would have been prohibited through the use of precise words. Therefore, the by-law was held to not prohibit the display of the election sign.

The dissenting judges found nothing in the provisions of the by-law which conflicted with the federal Elections Act. The by-law was of general application and was not aimed exclusively at federal election signs. Thus, although it incidentally prevented a particular form of political propaganda, it did not interfere with the working of Canadian parliamentary institutions.

19. *Ross v. Registrar of Motor Vehicles*
[1975] 1 S.C.R. 5, 42 D.L.R. (3d) 68

The plaintiff, R, was convicted of impaired driving under the Criminal Code, and as a consequence was prohibited from driving for six months except for driving to and from work between Monday and Friday. Section 238 of the Criminal Code said that a judge could make an order prohibiting the convicted driver "from driving a motor vehicle in Canada at all times or at such times and places as may be specified". The order stated that R's licence was not to be suspended. However, the defendant, RMV, suspended R's licence for a period of three months pursuant to s. 21 of the provincial Highway Traffic Act, which stated that a conviction for impaired driving carried an automatic suspension.

R instituted an action in the Supreme Court of Ontario for a declaration that s. 21 of the Highway Traffic Act was inoperativeand that the suspension of his licence was of no effect. A joint application was then made to remove the case to the Supreme Court of Canada to determine whether: (1) s. 21 of the Highway Traffic Act was valid; (2) s. 238 of the Criminal Code was *ultra vires*; and (3) s. 21 of the Highway Traffic Act was rendered inoperative by s. 238 of the Criminal Code.

A majority of the Supreme Court observed that the Criminal Code provided for prohibitory orders which were limited as to time and place. It was possible for the terms of such a limitation to correspond with a provincial licence suspension, in which case there was no conflict and both could operate simultaneously. Similarly, terms of a Criminal Code limitation might conflict with a provincial licence suspension, in which case the suspension could operate and the driver would not get the benefit of the limitation. In either case the two schemes were able to operate simultaneously, and both had been validly enacted. There was nothing in the Criminal Code authorizing the convicting magistrate to direct that R's licence not be suspended, so this part of the order was held to have been made without jurisdiction.

The dissenting judges held that both s. 21 of the Highway Traffic Act and s. 238 of the Criminal Code were valid legislation. However, since there was a conflict the federal legislation had to prevail such that the provincial suspension would be inoperative.

20. *Multiple Access Ltd. v. McCutcheon*
[1982] 2 S.C.R. 161, 138 D.L.R. (3d) 1

The appellant, MA, was a federally incorporated company. A shareholder action was initiated under the Ontario Securities Act against corporate insiders who were alleged to have engaged in insider trading. The Ontario Securities Act and the Canada Corporations Act contained almost identical provisions prohibiting insider trading. The insiders argued that since a proceeding under the federal Act was available (for which the limitation period had already expired), the proceeding under the provincial Act was of no effect. The trial judge held that the proceeding under the provincial Act was valid notwithstanding the federal provisions, but the Divisional Court and the Court of Appeal held that the doctrine of paramountcy prevented the operation of the provincial Act.

The Supreme Court of Canada construed the federal insider trading provisions as having both a securities law and a companies law aspect. Both aspects were considered to have equal importance, so that the provisions could be validly enacted by both the federal Parliament and the provincial Legislature. The provincial insider trading provisions were validly enacted as being in relation to property and civil rights in the province. Federal incorporation did not render a company immune from provincial securities regulation of general application.

The valid provisions of the federal statute did not render inoperative the valid provisions of the provincial Act. The provincial legislation duplicated the federal, but did not contradict it. Paramountcy would apply only in cases of actual conflict in operation, where compliance with one statute would result in non-compliance with the other. The two statutes could operate concurrently and therefore the provisions of the Ontario Securities Act were not rendered inoperative by the provisions of the Canada Corporations Act.

21. *Bank of Montreal v. Hall*
[1990] 1 S.C.R. 121, 65 D.L.R. (4th) 361

The respondent, H, defaulted on a loan secured by two real property mortgages granted in favour of the appellant, B. The bank seized a piece of H's farm machinery pursuant to the federal Bank Act, and brought an action to enforce its real property mortgage. H sought to have the proceedings dismissed by virtue of the fact that the bank had not served notice to seize under the provisions of the provincial Limitation of Civil Rights Act. The parties applied for a determination of the question whether a chartered bank was required to comply with the provincial Act in enforcing its rights under the federal Act.

The chambers judge held that the bank did not have to comply with the provincial Act, but the decision was reversed by the Court of Appeal. An appeal was taken to the Supreme Court of Canada on the issues of whether the relevant provisions of either the Limitations of Civil Rights Act or the Bank Act were *ultra vires*, and whether the Bank Act provisions rendered inoperative the provisions of the Limitation of Civil Rights Act.

The provisions of the Limitations of Civil Rights Act were held to be in relation to property and civil rights in the province, and were thus *intra vires* the provincial Legislature. With respect to the Bank Act, the Supreme Court rejected the argument that federal banking power could not extend to allow Parliament to define the procedures for enforcing a federal security interest. The provisions of the Bank Act creating the security interest were intended to provide a nationally uniform mechanism to facilitate access to capital without involving a widely varying set of provincial schemes. As such, Parliament had validly exercised its federal banking power, and the provisions were not *ultra vires*. Parliament had created a code which left no room for the operation of the provincial legislation, which was therefore to be construed as inapplicable to a security taken under the Bank Act.

The Court also considered the doctrine of paramountcy as defined in *Multiple Access Ltd. v. McCutcheon (20)* and determined that there was an actual conflict in operation between the federal and provincial legislation. Under the Bank Act a creditor would be entitled to seize its security upon default, whereas seizure under the Limitation of Civil Rights Act would be conditional on the decision of a judge. Compliance with the federal entailed defiance of the provincial, and compliance with the provincial was incompatible with federal legislative purpose.

22. *Starr v. Houlden*
[1990] 1 S.C.R. 1366, 68 D.L.R. (4th) 641

The appellant, S, was alleged to have made improper campaign contributions to several provincial cabinet ministers, and other members of the government had been accused of acting with S and the Tridel Corporation ("Tridel") to improperly divert public funds. The Province of Ontario appointed a commission of inquiry to investigate these activities. The terms of reference of the commission were to investigate the nature and extent of the dealings involving S and Tridel and public officials, and to inquire into and report upon any circumstances or dealings where there was sufficient evidence that a benefit was conferred on an elected or unelected public official. S and Tridel brought an application to challenge the province's jurisdiction to establish the commission, but the challenge was dismissed by both the Divisional Court and the Court of Appeal.

The Supreme Court of Canada looked to the pith and substance of the Order-in-Council establishing the inquiry by examining both its purpose and effect. Although a commission of inquiry may have a double aspect, a court might be able to identify a predominant feature that outweighs the competing incidental aspect. In this case, a majority of the Supreme Court concluded that the commission of inquiry was in pith and substance a substitute police investigation and preliminary inquiry into a specific offence under s. 121(1) of the Criminal Code. The only named parties were two private individuals and there was a "striking resemblance" between the terms of reference of the commission and s. 121(1) of the Criminal Code which supported the Court's conclusion. The establishment of such a commission was seen to interfere with federal interests in maintaining a criminal justice system, and was thus held to be *ultra vires* the province.

In dissent, L'Heureux-Dubé J. did not interpret the matter as an inquiry solely into a specific crime committed by specific named persons. In the context of the establishment of the commission, and upon a careful examination of its terms of reference, it had the wider function of examining conduct which may or may not have constituted a criminal offence. Because of this wider function L'Heureux-Dubé J. would have held the inquiry to be a valid exercise of provincial power to investigate a purely provincial matter.

Limitations on Legislative Powers

23. *R. v. Drybones*
[1970] S.C.R. 282, 9 D.L.R. (3d) 473

The respondent, D, was charged under s. 94 of the federal Indian Act with being intoxicated off a reserve. He was convicted by a magistrate but acquitted by the Territorial Court of the North West Territories. The acquittal was upheld by the Court of Appeal on the grounds that Indians had been denied equality before the law as contemplated by the Canadian Bill of Rights. The territorial Liquor Ordinance provided that no person shall be intoxicated in a public place, with the result that only an Indian could be guilty of the offence of being intoxicated in other than a public place.

Section 2 of the Bill of Rights stated that unless otherwise declared by an Act of Parliament, every law of Canada shall "be so construed and applied as not to abrogate, abridge or infringe" the rights and freedoms recognized therein. The Court of Appeal concluded that s. 94 of the Indian Act was rendered inoperative by this provision of the Bill of Rights.

A majority of the Supreme Court of Canada agreed with the Court of Appeal, rejecting the argument that the Bill of Rights merely provided a canon of construction for the interpretation of legislation. A declaration that a section of a statute is inoperative was seen to be analogous to a situation in which valid provincial legislation ceased to be operative by reason of conflicting federal legislation. Section 94 of the Indian Act was inconsistent with the right to equality as set out in the Bill of Rights, and thus was declared inoperative.

The dissenting judges held that it would require plain words byParliament to invite the courts to repeal legislation. Parliament instructed the courts to construe and apply laws in accordance with the principles enunciated in the Bill of Rights, but did not allow the courts to refuse to apply any law.

24. *Attorney General of Canada v. Lavell*
[1974] S.C.R. 1349, 38 D.L.R. (3d) 481

Under s. 12 of the Indian Act, an aboriginal woman lost her Indian status upon marrying a person who was not an Indian. However, there was no corresponding provision by which an aboriginal man with Indian status who married a non-Indian woman would lose his status. The respondent, L, belonged to an Indian band. When she married a non-Indian her name was removed from the Indian Register. The Registrar's decision was appealed to a judge and then to the Federal Court of Appeal, who held that the Canadian Bill of Rights rendered s. 12 inoperative. A second respondent, B, also married a non-Indian. She sought an injunction restraining the members of the Council from expelling her and her children from the reserve after her separation. The Supreme Court of Ontario held that s. 12 was inoperative. The Crown appealed both judgments to the Supreme Court of Canada.

Four members of the Court held that s. 12 of the Indian Act was passed by Parliament in discharge of its function to specify how and by whom Crown lands reserved for status Indians are to be used, and that the Bill of Rights could not render such legislationinoperative. Also, the Bill of Rights did not require federal legislation to be declared inoperative unless it offended one of the rights specifically guaranteed in s. 1 of the Bill of Rights, but a finding of discriminatory legislation afforded an added reason for rendering it ineffective. And, inequality before the law under the Bill of Rights meant equality of treatment in the enforcement and application of the laws of Canada, and no such inequality was a necessary result of the application of s. 12. *R. v. Drybones (23)* was distinguished on the ground that it did not concern the internal regulation of the lives of aboriginal peoples while on reserves. Pigeon J. wrote a concurring opinion in which he adopted his own dissenting opinion in **Drybones**.

Four dissenting judges applied the **Drybones** case to hold that if discrimination by reason of race rendered certain statutory provisions inoperative, then discrimination by reason of sex must lead to the same result.

The Crown's appeals were allowed with respect to both respondents.

25.   Hunter et al. v. Southam Inc.
        [1984] 2 S.C.R. 145, 9 C.R.R. 355

The appellant, H, Director of Investigation and Research of the Combines Investigation Branch, authorized several Combines Investigation officers to enter and examine documents at the business premises of a newspaper owned by the respondent, S. The authorization was given pursuant to subs. 10(1) of the Combines Investigation Act. In compliance with subs. 10(3) of the Act, a member of the Restrictive Trade Practices Commission certified the authorization. S sought an interlocutory injunction which was denied. An appeal to the Alberta Court of Appeal resulted in the decision that subs. 10(3) and by implication subs. 10(1) were inconsistent with s. 8 of the Charter of Rights and Freedoms guaranteeing the right to be secure against unreasonable search or seizure.

An appeal was taken to the Supreme Court of Canada where Dickson J. spoke for the full Court. He stated that the Charter of Rights and Freedoms is a purposive document intended to constrain government action rather than to authorize it. The purpose of s. 8 was to guarantee the individual's right to a reasonable expectation of privacy. The question of what is reasonable requires an assessment of the public's right to privacy balanced against the government's legitimate law enforcement goals.

The assessment required a purposive approach which sought to prevent an unjustified search rather than to allow a search and then determine whether or not it was justified. This would require a system of prior authorization rather than subsequent validation. Subsection 10(3) did establish a system of prior authorization.

The prior authorization would have to be given by someone able to assess the evidence of reasonableness in an entirely neutral and impartial manner. A member of the Restrictive Trade Practices Commission had investigatory functions which could interfere with the judicial functions exercised in the certification. Therefore, the authorization required by subs. 10(3) did not satisfy the requirements of s. 8 of the Charter.

The minimum standard for authorizing a search was reasonable and probable grounds, established upon oath, of belief that an offence had been committed and that evidence would be found at the place of the search. This standard was not met by the provisions of the Combines Investigation Act.

An argument that the appropriate standard should be read into the provisions was rejected. The legislative lacunae were left to be filled by the Legislature, and not the courts. Subsections 10(1) and 10(3) were held to be inconsistent with s. 8 of the Charter, and were thus of no force or effect.

26. *R. v. Big M Drug Mart Ltd.*
[1985] 1 S.C.R. 295, 13 C.R.R. 64

The respondent, B, was charged under the federal Lord's Day Act with selling goods on a Sunday. The Provincial Court Judge acquitted on the grounds that the Lord's Day Act could not be justified under Parliament's criminal law power under the Constitution Act, 1867, and that the Lord's Day Act infringed freedom of religion guaranteed in s. 2 of the Charter of Rights and Freedoms. The Court of Appeal unanimously upheld the validity of the Lord's Day Act under federal criminal law power, and by a majority held that the Act infringed the freedom of religion provision of the Charter.

On appeal to the Supreme Court of Canada, the Crown challenged the standing of B on the grounds that a corporation could not have a conscience or hold a religious belief. The Court rejected this argument, stating that an accused was entitled to defend a criminal charge by attacking the constitutional validity of the law under which the charge was brought. The Crown also objected to the jurisdiction of the Provincial Court to declare legislation invalid. This argument was also rejected as the Provincial Court was simply preventing the accused from being convicted under an invalid statute.

On the issue of constitutionality, the Court declared that both the purpose and the effect of the statute are relevant. A review of the historic underpinnings and case law led to the conclusion that the Lord's Day Act should be characterized as having the religious purpose of sabbatical observance, rather than the secular purpose of providing a uniform day of rest from labour. If such a purpose offended religious freedom it would be unnecessary to consider the effect of the Act, although it was observed that legislation with an unconstitutional purpose would likely have unconstitutional effects.

Interpreting the Charter by the purposive approach set out in *Hunter et al. v. Southam Inc. (25)*, the Court stated the purpose of freedom of conscience and religion to be that "government may not coerce individuals to affirm a specific religious belief or to manifest a specific religious practice for a sectarian purpose" (P. Macklem, R.C.B. Risk, C.J. Rogerson, *et al.*, *Canadian Constitutional Law*, Vol. II (Toronto: Emond Montgomery, 1994) p. 157). On that basis the compelled observance of the Christian Sabbath was held to infringe freedom of conscience and religion. The legislation was not saved under s. 1 of the Charter as being a reasonable limit because the argument to uphold the legislation was that there was value in having a universal day of rest from labour. However, it was disingenuous to accept a secular justification for legislation which was in pith and substance religious.

If the purpose of the legislation were secular it would come under the provincial power of property and civil rights. However, given the religious purpose of the Act, it was within the competence of Parliament under the criminal law power to safeguard public morals. Thus, although the Lord's Day Act had been validly enacted by the Federal Parliament it was of no force and effect by virtue of the Charter of Rights, and the Crown's appeal was dismissed.

The Judicial System

27. ***Crown Grain Co. v. Day***
[1908] A.C. 504 (P.C.)

The Manitoba Legislature enacted a statute in relation to liens in which it was provided that a judgment of the provincial court would be final and conclusive. This provision conflicted with the Supreme Court Act, which allowed appeals to the Supreme Court from any final judgment of the highest court of final resort in any province. The competency of the Supreme Court Act was challenged.

The appellant, C, maintained that it was an implied condition of the Supreme Court Act that the Supreme Court could have its jurisdiction circumscribed by provincial legislation in matters which were reserved to the provinces under the British North America Act. The Privy Council rejected this argument. Such matters covered such a wide area that to so limit the jurisdiction of the Supreme Court would be to defeat its main purposes. The establishment of a Court of Appeal for Canada properly belonged to the Dominion Parliament. However, even assuming that there was some overlap with provincial powers, the federal legislation would prevail. Therefore the validity of the Supreme Court Act was upheld and the appeal dismissed.

28. ***Attorney General of Ontario v. Attorney General of Canada (Validity of References Case)***
[1912] A.C. 571, 3 D.L.R. 509 (P.C)

The Supreme Court Act provided for references to the Supreme Court to answer important questions of law or fact concerning such matters as the interpretation of the British North America Act, the constitutionality of legislation, and the powers of the federal Parliament or provincial Legislatures. Under the Act it was the Court's duty to hear, consider and answer all questions so referred.

The provinces contended that no legislature in Canada had the right to pass an Act allowing for such references. It was argued that the power to ask questions of the Supreme Court was so wide in its terms that it grossly interfered with the judicial character of the Court, and as such gravely interfered with the rights of the provinces and individual citizens. The duty to answer questions was alleged to be incompatible with free access of litigants to an unbiased tribunal of appeal.

The Privy Council noted that, since the enactment of the Supreme Court Act, the Court had been asked and had answered several questions referred to it, some of which questions had been appealed to and disposed of by the Privy Council. Their Lordships considered that they would not have engaged in such a practice for so long if it subverted the independence and character of courts of justice in the manner proposed by the provinces. To entertain the appellant's arguments would be to comment on the wisdom or policy of the enactment, which was properly a matter for Parliament. Therefore, the appeal was dismissed.

29. *B.C. Power Corporation v. B.C. Electric Company*
[1962] S.C.R. 642, 34 D.L.R. (2d) 196 at 274

The plaintiff, BCP, a federal company, owned all the outstanding shares of the defendant, BCE, a provincial company. The British Columbia Legislature enacted legislation declaring the outstanding shares of the provincial company to be vested in the Crown in right of the Province. BCP brought an action against BCE and the Attorney General of B.C. for a declaration that the legislation was *ultra vires*.

Pending the outcome of the litigation and upon the application of the plaintiff, a judge appointed a receiver of the undertaking, property, and interests of the defendant. The defendant's appeal of the judge's decision was allowed by the Court of Appeal.

In the Supreme Court of Canada, the defendants contended that the judge had no jurisdiction to make a receivership order which would affect the property or interests of the Crown. However, eight members of the Court held that, in a federal system where Crown prerogatives are divided between the Dominion and the Provinces, neither the provincial nor the federal Crown could claim Crown immunity based on an interest in property where such interest depended solely on the validity of legislation which had been passed by the Crown itself. Just as the Court had jurisdiction to determine the validity of the legislation, it had jurisdiction to preserve assets whose title was dependent upon the validity of the legislation.

30. *Quebec North Shore Paper Company v. Canadian Pacific Limited*
[1977] 2 S.C.R. 1054, 9 N.R. 471

The respondent, C, contracted to build a rail car marine terminal for the appellant, Q. Two months before the terminal was to be completed, work had not started on it. Q alleged that they had fulfilled their obligations under the contracts but that

C was in default. Q brought an action in Federal Court for damages and resiliation of the contracts.

C challenged the jurisdiction of the Federal Court, saying that the action should have been brought in Quebec Superior Court. The contracts were to be interpreted and construed in accordance with the laws of Quebec since three of the four parties had their head offices in Quebec, and the contracts were entered into in Quebec. The jurisdictional challenge was rejected by the Federal Court Trial Division and the Federal Court of Appeal.

The Supreme Court of Canada unanimously allowed the appeal. Section 23 of the Federal Court Act granted jurisdiction to the Trial Division for claims for relief or a remedy "sought under an Act of the Parliament of Canada or otherwise in relation to" a specific class of subjects. This section was read in light of s. 101 of the British North America Act which allowed the Parliament of Canada to establish courts for "the better Administration of the Laws of Canada." The two sections were interpreted to mean that the claim for relief under s. 23 had to be sought under an applicable and existing federal law. In this case the action was not brought under any federal statute and the applicable law was that of the Province of Quebec.

31.   *R. v. Thomas Fuller Construction Co. (1958) Ltd. (Third Party) and Foundation Co. of Canada Ltd.*
    [1980] 1 S.C.R. 695, 106 D.L.R. (3d) 193

The original plaintiff, F, contracted with the federal Crown to construct a research centre. The Crown instructed the company to stop work due to foundation damage caused by blasting operations carried on by a subcontractor, Thomas Fuller. As a result of the delay F brought an action against the Crown in contract and in tort. The Crown issued a third party notice to the respondent, T, claiming indemnity and contribution under the Negligence Act of Ontario. On an application for directions a judge of the Trial Division of the Federal Court struck out the third party notice on the grounds that the claim was based on provincial law and not "federal law". The Federal Court of Appeal dismissed the Crown's appeal.

A majority of the Supreme Court of Canada considered the question to be whether federal law embraced the issues on the third party notice, and held that it did not. The main action was founded on the federal Crown Liability Act, but the third party claim arose out of contract and under the provincial Negligence Act. As a third party claim is a substantive proceeding and not a mere incident of the principal action, legislation giving jurisdiction over the claim in a main action does not extend to the claim for indemnity against a third party. The Crown's appeal was dismissed.

32. *Minister of Justice of Canada and Minister of Finance of Canada v. Borowski*
[1981] 2 S.C.R. 575, [1982] 1 W.W.R. 97

The respondent, B, brought an action against the appellants seeking a declaration that the provisions of the Criminal Code permitting therapeutic abortions were invalid as being contrary to the right to life provision of the Canadian Bill of Rights. The action was brought in the Saskatchewan Court of Queen's Bench. The appellants contested the jurisdiction of the court to hear the matter and denied that B had the necessary standing to maintain the action.

B brought a motion to establish the jurisdiction of the Queen's Bench. It was ordered that the Court did have jurisdiction and an appeal to the Court of Appeal was dismissed. A further appeal was brought to the Supreme Court of Canada on the issue of standing. B's statement of claim identified him as a citizen of Canada and a taxpayer to the Government of Canada, and it outlined the various means by which he protested the validity of the legislation.

A majority of the Supreme Court considered that due to the exculpatory nature of the legislation under attack, it did not directly affect or exceptionally prejudice any class of person who would have cause to attack it. But it did have a direct impact on unborn foetuses, hence the only way in which the validity of the legislation could be brought into court would be through some interested citizen. The Court held that for such a citizen to establish status to attack the legislation, that person "need only to show that he is affected by it directly or that he has a genuine interest as a citizen in the validity of the legislation and that there is no other reasonable and effective manner in which the issue may be brought before the Court" (at 575-76). B was held to have met this test, and the appeal was dismissed.

The dissenting judges held that B failed to establish any judicially cognizable interest in the matter and that such an important issue should not proceed in so abstract a manner as to have it litigated by B alone against two ministers of the Crown.

33. *Attorney General for Canada v. Law Society of British Columbia*
[1982] 2 S.C.R. 307, 137 D.L.R. (3d) 1

The respondent, L, initiated disciplinary proceedings against one of its members for advertising in a manner contrary to the provincial Law Society Act. The member brought an action in the Supreme Court of British Columbia for a declaration that the rulings and orders of L were null and void, and for an interlocutory injunction to restrain L from continuing with the disciplinary proceedings. The member alleged that the restrictions on advertising violated his right to free speech and contravened the provisions of the Combines Investigation Act.

L held the disciplinary proceedings, found the member guilty, and recommended suspension. The member obtained an order enjoining any action on the recommendation. Subsequently, the Director of Investigation and Research commenced an inquiry under the Combines Investigation Act into the conduct of L. L brought an action in the Supreme Court of the province seeking a declaration that the Combines Investigation Act was not applicable or, if it was applicable, it was *ultra vires* the Parliament of Canada. There was also an issue as to whether the Trial Division of the Federal Court had exclusive jurisdiction to grant declaratory relief in determining the constitutional applicability of the Combines Investigation Act to L.

The trial judge determined that the Combines Investigation Act did apply to L and that it was not *ultra vires*, and that the Federal Court did not have exclusive jurisdiction in the circumstances. The Court of Appeal found it unnecessary to decide whether the Combines Investigation Act was *ultra vires* because it did not apply to L. The Court of Appeal agreed that the jurisdiction of the British Columbia Supreme Court was not ousted by the Federal Court.

The Supreme Court of Canada found that L was discharging its duty, under a valid provincial statute, to govern the profession in the interest of the public, and not conspiring to lessen competition. Therefore, the Combines Investigation Act did not apply and it was unnecessary to decide whether or not it was *ultra vires*. As a consequence of the valid exercise of its powers, L was not violating the member's freedom of speech.

On the issue of the jurisdiction of the Federal Court, it was held that a statute establishing a Court "for the better administration of the laws of Canada" (Whyte, Lederman & Bur, p. 5-14) could not concurrently exclude the provincial superior courts from declaring a statute enacted by Parliament to be beyond the constitutional authority of Parliament. The provincial superior courts were organized by the provinces but presided over by federally appointed judges, and thus occupied a position of prime importance in the scheme of federal-provincial jurisdiction. To oust their jurisdiction as suggested would leave them with the task of executing both federal and provincial laws without being able to discriminate between those which were valid and those which were invalid, so as to refuse to execute the invalid ones.

Section 96 Courts

34. *Reference re Adoption Act*
[1938] S.C.R. 398, [1938] 3 D.L.R. 497

Four questions were referred to the Supreme Court of Canada in respect of four statutes of the Province of Ontario. The questions concerned the judges, magistrates, and justices of the peace identified in the various acts, and whether these officials had the authority to perform the functions vested in them by the Provincial Legislature.

There was no dispute that the subject matter of the four statutes was within provincial jurisdiction. The Court rejected the proposition that provincial legislatures could only appoint officers exercising solely ministerial functions, and that s. 96 of the British North America Act encompassed the appointment of judges and officers to all provincial courts. At the date of Confederation, magistrates and justices of the peace exercised jurisdiction in civil matters. By virtue of s. 129 of the British North America Act, such jurisdiction continued after Confederation for those officers not within s. 96. However, such jurisdiction was not fixed forever. It could be altered by provincial legislation as long as such legislation did not create a court within the scope of s. 96. On an examination of the statutes it was held that in every case the judicial officers identified therein did have the authority to perform the functions set out in the legislation.

35. *Toronto v. York Township*
    [1938] A.C. 415, [1938] 1 D.L.R. 593 (P.C.)

The appellant, T, and the respondent, Y, entered into an agreement whereby T supplied water to Y at an established rate of payment which could be altered by mutual settlement or by arbitration. Subsequently, the province passed the Township of York Act, 1936, which allowed either party to apply to the Ontario Municipal Board to vary the rates, notwithstanding the provisions of the agreement. The Municipal Board was given jurisdiction to hear the application and vary or fix the rates by a decision which was to be final with no appeal.

Y applied to vary the rates, and the Municipal Board ordered the City to permit inspection of their waterworks and to produce documents. The decision was affirmed by the Court of Appeal.

T appealed to the Privy Council, attacking the legislation on three grounds: (1) the Municipal Board was invalidly constituted as being a Superior Court; (2) the power to make the order in question could have been exercised only by a Superior Court; and (3) the Act was invalid as purporting to vest the jurisdiction of a Superior Court in the Municipal Board.

The Privy Council examined the legislative history of the Municipal Board Act to conclude that although the Board had been clothed with the functions of a court, it was in pith and substance an administrative body. The provisions were severable such that those purporting to constitute the Board as a Court of Justice analogous to a Superior, District or County Court were invalid. Examination, inspection and discovery of documents were valid administrative functions, and the Act in which those powers had been set out was validly enacted. Thus the order complained of was valid and the appeal was allowed.

36. *Labour Relations Board of Saskatchewan v. John East Iron Works Ltd.*
    [1949] A.C. 134, [1948] 4 D.L.R. 673 (P.C.)

The United Steel Workers of America applied to the appellant L for reinstatement of six individuals that had been dismissed from their employment with respondent J. L found discrimination under the Trade Union Act and ordered J to reinstate the employees and to pay them what they would have earned if they had not been dismissed. J applied to quash the orders of L, alleging that the Trade Union Act was *ultra vires* in so far as it purported to set up a "Superior, District or County Court or tribunal analogous thereto" (Macklem, Risk, Rogerson, *et al.*, p. 422). The Saskatchewan Court of Appeal upheld the challenge and quashed the orders of the Board.

The Privy Council viewed the question as being whether the Board exercised a judicial power in making its orders. If not, that was the end of the matter. However, the Court declined to decide that question and instead found that the jurisdiction exercisable by the Board was not such as to constitute it a court within s. 96 of the British North America Act.

The Saskatchewan Court of Appeal concluded that the Board exercised a judicial power analogous to courts in the sense that courts could enforce employment contracts. However the Privy Council saw this view as too narrow. The question was to be determined in light of the conception of industrial relations whereby reinstatement of the employee was "the means by which labour practices regarded as unfair are frustrated and the policy of collective bargaining as a road to industrial peace is secured" (Whyte, Lederman & Bur, p. 5-53).

The judicial function involved individuals pursuing their own rights on their own behalf, whereas before the Board the individual's rights could be advanced by some other party on behalf of a group of individuals. Further, the constitution of the Board was to be equally represented by labour and management, which distinguished it from a s. 96 court. And, the fact that there was no appeal or review available from a decision of the Board did not lead to the conclusion that it was analogous to a court. The appeal was allowed.

37. *Re Supreme Court Act Amendment Act 1964 (B.C.)*
    Attorney General of B.C. v. McKenzie
    [1965] S.C.R. 490, 51 D.L.R. (2d) 623

The judges of the County Courts as local judges of the Supreme Court of British Columbia were granted jurisdiction to exercise powers under several Acts, including the Divorce and Matrimonial Causes Act. This jurisdiction was granted by the Supreme Court Act Amendment Act, whose validity was challenged on the grounds that it conflicted with the federal power of legislating with respect to marriage and divorce, and that it purported to authorize judicial appointments required to be made by the Governor General. On a reference to the British Columbia Court of Appeal, the Supreme Court Act Amendment Act was held to be *ultra vires* the British Columbia Legislature.

The Supreme Court of Canada observed that the provincial Legislature was precluded from making substantive changes to the law of divorce in B.C., but held that the legislation in question did not make any such changes. Since the Dominion Parliament had not passed legislation providing for the establishment of courts for the administration of marriage and divorce in B.C., it was within the competence of the provincial Legislature to do so.

This was seen to be a case of the province regulating the administration of justice within a province by prescribing the jurisdiction to be exercised by provincial courts presided over by federally appointed judges. The legislation did not offend ss. 96 to 101 of the British North America Act and thus the appeal was allowed.

38. *Seminary of Chicoutimi v. Attorney General and Minister of Justice of Quebec*
[1973] S.C.R. 681, 27 D.L.R. (3d) 356

The original respondent, City of Chicoutimi, adopted a by-law under which the appellant, S, was subject to property tax assessment. S sought to quash the by-law on grounds of illegality by applying to the Provincial Court, formerly the Magistrate's Court. Provincial legislation had transferred jurisdiction over challenges of by-laws from the Superior Court to the Magistrate's Court.

The respondent, A, attacked the legislation as being *ultra vires* the provincial Legislature because it transferred to a provincial Court a matter which came under the jurisdiction of judges appointed under s. 96 of the British North America Act, that being petitions to quash municipal by-laws on grounds of illegality and not merely on grounds of procedural irregularity.

The trial judge proceeded to hear the petition and quashed the by-law. The Court of Appeal held the provincial legislation to be *ultra vires* and held that the provincial Court did not have jurisdiction.

The Supreme Court of Canada reviewed the history of the courts to conclude that the jurisdiction conferred by the legislation in question was not generally in conformity with the kind of jurisdiction exercised in 1867 by the courts of summary jurisdiction, but conformed rather to the kind of jurisdiction exercised by s. 96 courts. As such, the legislation was held to be *ultra vires* and the appeal was dismissed.

39. *Reference re Residential Tenancies Act, 1979*
[1981] 1 S.C.R. 714, 123 D.L.R. (3d) 554

The Ontario Legislature enacted the Residential Tenancies Act, 1979, establishing a code to govern landlords and tenants. The Residential Tenancy Commission was a tribunal set up to enforce the provisions of the Act. A reference to the Ontario Court of Appeal considered whether the Provincial Legislature had the authority to: (1) allow the Residential Tenancy Commission to make an order evicting a tenant, and (2) allow the Residential Tenancy Commission to make orders requiring landlords and tenants to comply with obligations imposed under the Act. The Court of Appeal held that the Provincial Legislature had no such authority.

The Supreme Court of Canada observed that since there is no general separation of powers in the Constitution, the Legislature of Ontario could confer non-judicial functions on courts, and judicial functions on non-courts, subject to s. 96 of the British North America Act. To determine the application of s. 96 a three-step test was formulated.

Step one was an inquiry into the particular power or jurisdiction conferred on the tribunal in light of the historical conditions existing at Confederation. A landlord seeking to evict a tenant or to enforce compliance orders in 1867 was seen to be in substantially the same position as a landlord seeking similar remedies under the Residential Tenancies Act. Thus, the powers conferred by the Act were held to be analogous or in broad conformity with the kind of powers historically exercised by the superior, county or district courts.

As a result of the finding of conformity it was necessary to proceed to step two, which involved consideration of the function within its institutional setting to determine if the function could still be considered to be "judicial". The Residential Tenancy Commission had the authority to hear and determine disputes between parties, but was not free to intervene. It applied relevant law and came to a decision which had the force of law. The Court concluded that the powers of the Commission, when viewed in their institutional setting, were essentially judicial.

The characterization of the powers as judicial led to step three, an examination of the Commission's impugned powers in relation to all of the Commission's powers conferred under the Act. Prior to the Residential Tenancies Act, three separate bodies were responsible for advisory, administrative, and adjudicative functions in relation to landlord and tenant law. The Act had the effect of consolidating these three functions under one body, the Residential Tenancy Commission. The Court held that the central function of the Commission was dispute resolution. As such the Act attempted to transfer the jurisdiction of Superior Courts to a provincially appointed tribunal. Therefore the powers in question violated s. 96, and the appeal was dismissed.

Delegation of Legislative Powers

40. *Attorney General of Nova Scotia v. Attorney General of Canada*
(Inter-delegation Case)
[1951] S.C.R. 31, [1950] 4 D.L.R. 369

The Lieutenant-Governor-in-Council of the Province of Nova Scotia referred to the Supreme Court of the Province the question of the constitutional validity of a bill entitled "An Act respecting the delegation of jurisdiction from the Parliament of Canada to the Legislature of Nova Scotia and *vice versa*".

The bill, if enacted, would have permitted the Lieutenant-Governor-in-Council to delegate to and withdraw from Parliament authority to legislate in relation to employment matters within the exclusive jurisdiction of the provinces as set out in s. 92 of the British North America Act (the "BNA Act"). In situations where Parliament had delegated to the Provincial Legislature authority to legislate in relation to employment matters within federal jurisdiction, the Lieutenant-Governor-in-Council would have been given authority to apply the provisions of any such Act by proclamation, and to raise revenue for provincial purposes by imposing a retail sales tax.

A majority of the Supreme Court of Nova Scotia held that the legislation was beyond the competence of the Provincial Legislature.

The Supreme Court of Canada dismissed the appeal. The legislation would have the effect of allowing the Canadian Parliament and theNova Scotia Legislature to make laws concerning matters not attributed to them by the constitution, thereby defeating the scheme of the constitution. The Parliament of Canada and the Provincial Legislatures, though sovereign, could only exercise the legislative powers granted to them by ss. 91 and 92 of the BNA Act. There was no express power of delegation, and jurisdiction could not be conferred by consent. Delegation to subordinate agencies was permissible, but neither Parliament nor the Legislatures could "abdicate their powers and invest for the purpose of legislation, bodies which by the very terms of the BNA Act are not empowered to accept such delegation" (at S.C.R. 44).

41. *P.E.I. Potato Marketing Board v. Willis*
[1952] 2 S.C.R. 392, [1952] 4 D.L.R. 146

The Prince Edward Island Legislature enacted the Agricultural Products Marketing Act. The Act conferred authority on the Lieutenant-Governor-in-Council to establish schemes for regulation within the province of marketing of natural products. Marketing boards were set up to administer the Act. The P.E.I. Potato Marketing Board ("PEIPMB") was set up to fix and collect licence fees.

There was also a federal Agricultural Products Marketing Act. By Order-in-Council under that Act, the PEIPMB was granted similar powers in relation to marketing of potatoes as those granted under the provincial statute. A reference to the Supreme Court of Prince Edward Island considered whether Parliament had jurisdiction to enact the Agricultural Products Marketing Act, and whether the Order-in-Council was valid. The court held the Act to be *ultra vires* and did not answer the question concerning the Order-in-Council.

The Supreme Court of Canada allowed the appeal. Parliament had legislated with respect to interprovincial trade as it was allowed to do. It was also allowed to authorize the Governor-in-Council to confer upon the PEIPMB the power to regulate marketing outside the province. Federal legislation did not confer any additional powers to the provincial legislature, it vested certain powers in a group of individuals. It did not matter that the same individuals had been appointed by the province to regulate marketing within the province. As such the legislation was valid. And, since the Order-in-Council was a valid exercise of the powers conferred on the Governor-in-Council by the federal Act, the order in council and the delegation of powers thereunder were valid.

42. *Lord's Day Alliance v. Attorney General of British Columbia*
[1959] S.C.R. 497, 19 D.L.R. (2d) 97

Section 6 of the federal Lord's Day Act made it unlawful to attend at or engage in any public contest for gain on a Sunday, "except as provided in any provincial Act or law". A provincial bill entitled "An Act to Amend the 'Vancouver Charter'" proposed to make such activities lawful for limited hours on a Sunday. The constitutionality of the bill was referred to the British Columbia Court of Appeal, who held by a majority that it was *intra vires*.

The Supreme Court of Canada dismissed the appeal. The relevant section of the provincial law governed the conduct of people on Sunday but did not create an offence against the criminal law. The legislation was permissive rather than prohibitory, and within the power of the Provincial Legislature as relating to property and civil rights or matters of a local nature.

Parliament chose to limit the operation of the Lord's Day Act. The Provincial Legislature took advantage of that limitation by exercising powers derived from s. 92 of the British North America Act. Therefore, it was not a case of delegation in which Parliament attempted to authorize a legislature to do something beyond its power.

43. *Coughlin v. Ontario Transport Highway Board*
[1968] S.C.R. 569, 68 D.L.R. (2d) 384

The appellant, C, carried on the business of interprovincial transport of goods. A licence was issued in Ontario to C under the federal Motor Vehicle Transport Act.

The respondent, O, sought to review the terms of the certificate which led to the issue of the licence. C applied for an order of prohibition to prevent O's review, on the ground that the Motor Vehicle Transport Act was *ultra vires*. Section 3 of the Act permitted the provincial transport board in each province to issue a licence to operate an extraprovincial undertaking within the province as though it were a local undertaking. The application for prohibition was dismissed by both the judge and the Court of Appeal.

In the Supreme Court of Canada, C contended that s. 3 was an unlawful delegation by Parliament to the Provincial Legislatures of the power to legislate in respect of interprovincial transport. A majority of the Court held that there was no delegation of law-making power. Parliament, in the exercise of its exclusive power, adopted the legislation of another body, which it was entitled to do. O derived its power to regulate interprovincial carriage of goods from Parliament, not from the Provincial Legislature. Therefore there was no unlawful delegation and the appeal was dismissed.

The dissenting judges felt that under the Act Parliament purported to relinquish all control over a field in which it had exclusive jurisdiction, and left the regulation of licensing to provincial authority.

DISTRIBUTION OF POWERS

Peace, Order and Good Government

44. ***Russell v. The Queen***
(1882), 7 App. Cas. 829 (P.C.)

The appellant, R, had been convicted of selling intoxicating liquors in contravention of the Canada Temperance Act, 1878. The Act set out a procedure by which individual counties or cities could choose to adopt and bring into force the provisions of the Act restricting liquor traffic. R applied for *certiorari* to quash the conviction on the ground that the legislation was invalid. The legislation and the conviction were upheld by the Supreme Court of New Brunswick. R appealed to the Privy Council.

R contended that the subject matter of the legislation was within provincial jurisdiction under one of three classes of subjects enumerated in s. 92 of the British North America Act: (1) saloon licences to raise revenue for local purposes; (2) property and civil rights in the province; and (3) matters of a merely local or private nature in the province.

The Privy Council dismissed the appeal. The Act was not intended to raise revenue and therefore was not within provincial jurisdiction as being a law in relation to saloon licensing.

The Act also did not fall within the subject matter of property and civil rights in the province. Although property was affected incidentally, the true nature of the legislation was promotion of public order and safety.

The fact that the prohibitory sections of the Act could be adopted at the option of individual counties and cities did not render it legislation in respect of local matters. Parliament had declared its object as being uniform legislation in all the provinces respecting traffic in liquor, with a view to promoting temperance. These objects were general and not local.

Since the legislation did not come within any of the classes of subjects assigned to the provinces, the legislation was held to be valid under Parliament's general power to make laws for the "peace, order and good government of Canada". The Privy Council thus chose not to decide whether the legislation fell within any of the classes of subject specifically assigned to Parliament.

45. *Attorney General for Ontario v. Attorney General for Canada (Local Prohibition Case)*
[1896] A.C. 348 (P.C.)

Seven questions were referred to the Supreme Court of Canada concerning federal and provincial legislation in relation to the sale of liquor. The Temperance Act, 1864 was enacted in Upper Canada and in force at Confederation. The Canada Temperance Act, 1886 repealed the prohibitory clauses of the Temperance Act, 1864. To restore to the municipalities the powers to make prohibitory by-laws, the Province of Ontario in 1890 enacted the Act to Improve the Liquor Licence Acts.

In the appeal from the Supreme Court of Canada, the Privy Council focused on the seventh question, that being whether the Ontario Legislature had jurisdiction to enact s. 18 of the 1890 Act, which allowed local councils to pass by-laws prohibiting the sale of liquor. Their Lordships first considered whether Parliament had jurisdiction to enact the Canada Temperance Act, and then if so, whether the Ontario Legislature was competent to enact s. 18.

Parliament was able to enact laws for the peace, order and good government of Canada even if the law was not in relation to any of the classes of subjects enumerated in s. 91 of the British North America Act. However, in doing so, Parliament had no authority to encroach upon any class of subjects assigned to the provincial legislatures by s. 92. Such legislation had to be strictly confined to matters that were unquestionably of Canadian interest and importance.

In this case, the Canada Temperance Act was held not to be in relation to any of the classes of subjects in s. 91, and specifically was not an act for the regulation of trade and commerce. However, on the authority of *Russell v. The Queen (44)*, the Act was held to be within Parliament's power to make laws for peace, order and good government.

The power of the province to restrict liquor traffic could have been supported by s. 92 under property and civil rights or matters of a local nature, however it was argued that Parliament hadoccupied the field by enacting the Canada Temperance Act. The Privy Council responded to this argument by recognizing that while valid federal legislation would override provincial legislation, Parliament had no authority to repeal any provincial statute. Therefore, it was not within the authority of Parliament to attempt to repeal the provisions of the 1864 Act by passing the Canada Temperance Act.

The Privy Council then considered the extent to which the Canada Temperance Act conflicted with the 1890 provincial Act. Application of the provisions of the two Acts would have led to significantly different results. However, neither statute was imperative. The prohibitory sections of both statutes did not apply until voluntarily adopted by a district or municipality, so they could co-exist without repugnancy. Thus it was held that the Ontario Legislature had jurisdiction to enact s. 18 subject to the qualification that its provisions would be inoperative in any district adopting the prohibitory sections of the Canada Temperance Act.

46. *In re The Board of Commerce Act, 1919*
[1922] 1 A.C. 191 (P.C.)

The Board of Commerce Act set up a Board which was to administer the Combines and Fair Prices Act. The latter statute involved investigation of combines, monopolies, trusts and mergers. The Board was empowered to prevent the formation of combines and prohibit the accumulation of certain "necessaries of life", which included food, clothing and fuel. The Board had made an order declaring that certain retail dealers had made an unfair profit on clothing.

Two questions were referred to the Supreme Court of Canada as to whether the Board had the authority to make the order, and whether the Board had the authority to require the Registrar of the Supreme Court of Ontario to cause the order to be made a rule of that court. A six-member panel of the Supreme Court split evenly on the validity of the legislation.

The Privy Council held that the legislation was in relation to property and civil rights in the province, and thus could not be upheld by either the trade and commerce or criminal law provisions of s. 91 of the British North America Act. Under exceptional circumstances, such as war, the subject matter of the legislation might have become of such paramount and overriding national importance as to allow the Dominion Parliament to intervene using its power to legislate for the peace, order and good government of the Dominion. However, the legislation in question was passed in 1919, after the war, so it was not intended to govern wartime conditions. In the absence of exceptional circumstances the Board had no power to make the order, and thus the second question did not arise.

47. *Fort Frances Pulp and Power Co. v. Manitoba Free Press*
[1923] A.C. 695 (P.C.)

The appellant, F, manufactured newsprint, and the respondent, M, published newspapers. M brought an action against F to recover amounts paid for paper at controlled prices pursuant to an order of the Paper Control Tribunal (the "Tribunal"). The Tribunal had been set up under federal legislation to hear appeals from orders of the Controller, who had the power to fix paper prices and quantities. The Tribunal made an order fixing a price for a certain period and directing F to refund any sums received in excess of the fixed prices. The trial judge gave judgment for M. The decision was upheld by the Appeal Division of the Supreme Court and the Ontario Court of Appeal. The Court of Appeal held that F was bound by its contracts, and thus did not address the issue of the validity of the order.

After World War I the Dominion Parliament enacted legislation confirming and extending the authority of the Controller and the Tribunal to allow them to complete all investigations and determine all matters remaining incomplete at the time of declaration of peace. All powers were to cease upon resolution of the outstanding matters. In order to dispose of this appeal the Privy Council assessed the validity of this legislation together with the War Measures Act, which allowed the Governor-in-Council to make such orders as deemed necessary for the security of the country in times of war.

The Court held that the legislation in question involved property and civil rights in the province and normally would have been beyond the competence of Parliament. However, the national emergency arising out of war concerned the peace, order and good government of the country and thus Parliament was empowered to deal with the emergency. Such an occurrence did not repeal the powers granted to the provinces under s. 92, but rather recognized the emergence of a new aspect of the business of government.

After the war an Order-in-Council had repealed all orders and regulations derived from the operation of the War Measures Act, with the exception of certain measures concerning consequential conditions arising out of the war. The control of paper was seen to involve such conditions, and therefore the order fixing and refunding the paper prices was valid. The appeal was dismissed.

48.   *Toronto Electric Commissioners v. Snider*
       [1925] A.C. 396 (P.C.)

The Dominion Parliament enacted the Industrial Disputes Investigation Act to enable the resolution of disputes between employers and employees concerning an extensive array of employment issues. Subsequently the Province of Ontario enacted the Trade Disputes Act covering matters similar to those of the federal Statute.

The respondent, S, was a member of a Board of Conciliation appointed under the Dominion Act. The appellant, T, was a public utility commission incorporated under provincial law. A dispute between S and several of its employees was brought before T. T brought an action in the Supreme Court of Ontario to restrain the proceedings on the ground that the federal legislation was *ultra vires*. An injunction was granted at trial but the decision was reversed by the Ontario Court of Appeal.

The Privy Council observed that the provincial legislation was valid under s. 92 of the British North America Act as being in relation to property and civil rights in the province. As such the federal legislation, relating to the same subject matter, could only be upheld if it fell within the provisions of s. 91. It was not supportable under any of the specific enumerated heads of s. 91, therefore it was necessary to determine whether it could be supported under the general power in relation to peace, order and good government.

The Privy Council concurred with the dissenting opinion of the Court of Appeal, in which it was stated that the Act could not be supported as dealing with an emergency or a matter of general national interest and importance. There was no national emergency in existence when the Statute was enacted, and it was not framed so as to come into operation during an emergency. The control of industrial disputes may have had national importance, but the means of dealing with such disputes involved the management of civil rights at a local level. The federal Act was therefore invalid and the appeal was allowed.

49.   *A.G. British Columbia v. A.G. Canada (The Natural Products*
       Marketing Act)
       [1937] A.C. 377, [1937] 1 D.L.R. 691 (P.C.)

The Natural Products Marketing Act was enacted by Parliament. It provided for the establishment of a Dominion Marketing Board which had regulatory powers relating to the quality, quantity, grade, class and manner of distribution of the marketing of natural products. The Act also provided for the establishment of an investigatory committee regarding such things as production costs, wages, prices and trade practices. A reference was brought to the Supreme Court of Canada to determine whether the Act was *intra vires* Parliament.

The Supreme Court of Canada held the legislation to be invalid. For the Court, Duff C.J. said that the enactment purported to regulate not only external and interprovincial trade, but local trade as well. The attempted regulation of local trade was so extensive that it could not be interpreted as being merely incidental to the regulation of external or interprovincial trade. Therefore, the Act could not be supported under the power to regulate trade and commerce under s. 91 of the British North America Act. Furthermore, Duff C.J. relied on *In re the Board of Commerce Act, 1919 (46)*, *Fort Frances Pulp and Power Co. v. Manitoba Free Press (47)*, and *Toronto Electric Commissioners v. Snyder (48)* to hold that the enactment could not be upheld under the power to legislate for peace, order and good government.

On appeal, the Privy Council agreed with the assessment of Duff C.J. holding the legislation to be *ultra vires*, and the appeal was dismissed.

50. *Attorney General for Ontario v. Canada Temperance Federation* [1946] A.C. 193 (P.C.)

Part II of the Canada Temperance Act, 1927 prohibited the sale of liquor in the areas in which the Act had been brought into force. Part I of the Act set out the procedure by which Part II would be brought into force, and Part III set out the penalties for breach. A question as to the constitutional validity of these parts of the Act was referred to the Ontario Court of Appeal, who decided that the provisions were *intra vires*.

On appeal to the Privy Council, the appellants contended that *Russell v. The Queen (44)*, upon which the Court of Appeal based its decision, was wrongly decided and ought to be overruled. The Court observed that the *Russell* case, which upheld the validity of the Canada Temperance Act, 1878, had stood unreversed for 63 years and had received express approval in subsequent decisions of the Privy Council. However, in *Toronto Electric Commissioners v. Snider (48)*, the *Russell* case was interpreted as being decided on its specific facts where the legislation was upheld as being in response to a national menace. In the present case the Privy Council viewed this explanation as being too narrow, saying that there was no suggestion that *Russell* was decided on the basis of emergency power. The Privy Council went on to say at 205 A.C. that:

> [t]he true test must be found in the real subject matter of the legislation: if it is such that it goes beyond local or provincial concern or interests and must from its inherent nature be the concern of the Dominion as a whole . . . then it will fall within the competence of the Dominion Parliament as a matter affecting the peace, order and good government of Canada, though it may in another aspect touch on matters specially reserved to the provincial legislatures.

The appellant, A, further argued that the 1927 Act was new legislation requiring the existence of circumstances to support it, and since such circumstances did not exist the new Act was *ultra vires*. This argument was rejected. Once it had been decided that the 1878 Act was valid, any Act which replaced it and consolidated it with subsequent amending Acts was equally valid. Therefore the Privy Council refused to strike down the validity of the *Russell* case or of the Dominion legislation, and the appeal was dismissed.

51. *Johannesson v. West St. Paul*
[1952] 1 S.C.R. 292, [1951] 4 D.L.R. 609

The appellant, J, operated a charter air service. He intended to build a facility to repair and service light and medium weight planes. To effect these intentions he and his wife acquired an option to purchase a piece of property in the Rural Municipality of West St. Paul. Before the transaction was completed the respondent W enacted a by-law pursuant to the provincial Municipal Act. Under the by-law, aerodromes or any places where aeroplanes would be kept for hire or gain were prohibited within the Municipality. J applied to have the Municipal Act and the by-law declared *ultra vires*. The application was dismissed at trial and by the Court of Appeal.

In the Supreme Court of Canada, five judges delivered opinions on behalf of a seven-member panel, unanimously allowing the appeal. The Privy Council in *Re Regulation and Control of Aeronautics (85)* held that legislation in relation to aeronautics was within the exclusive jurisdiction of Parliament. Aeronautics was seen to be a matter of national interest and importance such that Parliament could use its power to legislate for peace, order and good government. The nature of the legislation in question, regulating land use within a province, could not be segregated from aerial navigation as a whole. The province therefore had no jurisdiction and the by-law was *ultra vires*.

52. *Munro v. National Capital Commission*
[1966] S.C.R. 663, 57 D.L.R. (2d) 753

Pursuant to the National Capital Act, the respondent, N, expropriated a farm of 195 acres belonging to the appellant, M. N filed with the Exchequer Court an information offering $200,000 in compensation. M filed a statement of defence seeking a declaration that the expropriation was illegal on the ground that it was *ultra vires* Parliament to grant to N powers of expropriation. In the alternative M sought compensation of $420,000. The Exchequer Court held that the expropriation was valid.

In the Supreme Court of Canada it was argued that the land was expropriated for the purpose of establishing a Green Belt in the National Capital Region. Therefore, the power of expropriation was in the nature of zoning regulations contemplated by the Planning Acts of the provinces. As such, the National Capital Act was *ultra vires* in so far as it purported to confer such power on N.

The Supreme Court considered that the subject matter of the Act was the establishment of the National Capital Region as a region consisting of the seat of the Government of Canada and the surrounding area. It was to be developed, conserved, and improved "in order that the nature and character of the seat of the Government of Canada may be in accordance with its national significance" (Whyte, Lederman & Bur, p. 7-69). Such subject matter was not referred to in either s. 91 or s. 92 of the British North America Act. Therefore, it was necessary to determine whether the subject matter went beyond local or provincial interests to allow Parliament to exercise its power to legislate for peace, order and good government. The Court adopted the words of the trial judge who described the Act as dealing with "a single matter of national concern". Therefore, the legislation was held to be valid and the appeal was dismissed.

53. *Jones v. Attorney General for New Brunswick*
[1975] 2 S.C.R. 182, 45 D.L.R. (3d) 583

Subsection 14(1) of the Official Languages of New Brunswick Act provided that in any proceeding before a court, any person giving evidence could do so in the official language of that person's choice. Subsection 14(2) gave the court the power to order that the proceedings be conducted totally or partially in one of the official languages. Section 23C of the Evidence Act of New Brunswick allowed a judge to order proceedings to be conducted in any language where all the parties and their counsel had sufficient knowledge of the language.

Subsection 11(1) of the federal Official Languages Act provided that every court had the duty to ensure that any person giving evidence be heard in the language of that person's choice. Subsection 11(3) provided that in any criminal matter, any court could order that the proceedings be conducted in one of the official languages. Subsection 11(4) provided that subss. 11(1) and 11(3) did not apply to any court in which the use of either official language was permissible by virtue of s. 133 of the British North America Act (the "BNA Act"). Section 133 permitted the use of either official language by any person in any process issuing from any court established under the BNA Act, and from any of the courts of Quebec.

A reference was brought to the Appeal Division of the Supreme Court of New Brunswick regarding the validity and application of the various provisions.

The Appeal Division upheld the validity of both federal and provincial legislation, but held that s. 23C of the Evidence Act did not make subss. 11(1) and 11(3) of the Official Languages Act operative in New Brunswick. The appellant, J, was declared to be a person entitled to be heard on the reference. He appealed the decision to uphold the legislation and the respondent AG cross-appealed on the answers given to the questions.

The Supreme Court of Canada held the Official Languages Act to be valid. The appellant's submission that s. 133 of the BNA Act exhausted constitutional authority in relation to official languages was not supportable by the language of the section itself or by the scheme of distribution of powers under the Act generally. Section 91(1) of the BNA Act restricted the power of Parliament to amend the Constitution as regards the use of the English or French language. The argument that this section created a substantive limitation beyond that prescribed in s. 133 was untenable. The Official Languages Act in general, being limited to the purposes and institutions of the Parliament and Government of Canada, was within the legislative competence of Parliament as being a law for the peace, order and good government of Canada. The specific provisions of the Act with respect to court proceedings were supportable under Parliament's criminal law power and the power to provide for Courts for the better administration of the laws of Canada.

The provincial Evidence Act and Official Languages Act were upheld on the basis of s. 92(14) of the BNA Act, granting the provinces the power to legislate in respect of administration of justice. Section 23C of the Evidence Act rendered subss. 11(1) and 11(3) of the Official Languages Act operative in New Brunswick.

Therefore the appeal on the validity of the legislation was dismissed and the cross-appeal on the applicability of the legislation in the province was allowed.

54. *Reference re Anti-Inflation Act*
[1976] 2 S.C.R. 373, 68 D.L.R. (3d) 452

The Parliament of Canada introduced a bill which was to become the Anti-Inflation Act. The statute set up a scheme of wage and price controls that was binding both on the federal public sector and on specified private sector firms. It was not binding on the provincial public sector, but each provincial government could enter into an agreement with the federal government to have the Act apply. The Lieutenant-Governor-in-Council of the Province of Ontario authorized an order executing an agreement with the federal government to have the Act apply to the Ontario public sector.

A reference was directed to the Supreme Court of Canada to determine whether the legislation was *ultra vires*, and whether the intergovernmental agreement between Canada and Ontario was valid.

The Court unanimously held that the agreement was invalid. The Act provided that a federal Minister could enter into an agreement with the government of a province to have its provisions apply to the provincial public sector. However, it did not specify how or on what authority the provincial government would execute such an agreement. If the agreement were valid it would have the effect of altering the law of Ontario and precluding any future changes found to be inconsistent with the sanctions and guidelines imposed by the Act. The Provincial

Crown would have been legislating by proclamation, without any authority from the provincial Legislative Assembly.

The argument to support the validity of the legislation was advanced under two heads: the containment of inflation was a matter of national interest, and there was an existing or apprehended economic crisis amounting to an emergency. Laskin, C.J. for four members of the Court decided that the legislation was valid as "crisis legislation", being for the peace, order and good government of Canada. The judges looked at extrinsic evidence such as the Consumer Price Index to conclude that Parliament had a rational basis for regarding the Act as a measure which was temporarily necessary to address an economic crisis. Parliament's authority to act as it did was supported by its jurisdiction over monetary policy and regulation of trade and commerce. It was therefore unnecessary to consider the national interest argument.

For the two members of the court holding the legislation to be *ultra vires*, Beetz J. said of the containment of inflation:

> It is an aggregate of several subjects some of which form a substantial part of provincial jurisdiction. It is totally lacking in specificity. It is so pervasive that it knows no bounds. Its recognition as a federal head of power would render most provincial powers nugatory.
>
> (Macklem, Risk, Rogerson, *et al.*, pp. 249-50)

Therefore, the legislation could not be supported under the national dimensions doctrine. It was further held that Parliament did not purport to enact the legislation to deal with a national emergency. The Act was therefore invalid insofar as it applied to the provincial private sector. However, since severability was not pleaded, the Act as a whole was held to be *ultra vires*.

For the remaining three members of the Court, Ritchie J. stated that the validity of the legislation depended on whether it was enacted to combat a national emergency. It did not rest upon the national dimensions doctrine, because unless a national concern is made manifest by a national emergency, "[p]arliament is not endowed under the cloak of the "peace, order and good government" clause with the authority to legislate in relation to matters reserved to the Provinces under s. 92 of the British North America Act, 1867" (Macklem, Risk, Rogerson, *et al.*, p. 245). Although neither the preamble nor any of the provisions of the Act specifically declared a national emergency, a reading of the federal Government's white paper on the subject of inflation made it clear that Parliament was responding to an economic crisis. Therefore, the legislation was valid.

55. *R. v. Crown Zellerbach Canada Limited*
[1988] 1 S.C.R. 401, 49 D.L.R. (4th) 161

The respondent, C, was charged with dumping materials into the sea contrary to the federal Ocean Dumping Control Act. The definition of "the sea" included the internal waters of Canada other than fresh waters. The relevant section of the Act prohibited dumping except in accordance with the terms and conditions of a permit. C had a permit to dump waste from its logging operations at a site about two miles from where the waste was actually dumped. C conceded that Parliament had jurisdiction to regulate dumping in waters beyond provincial territorial limits, to regulate dumping in provincial waters to prevent pollution that would be harmful to fisheries, and to regulate the dumping in provincial waters of substances that would pollute extraprovincial waters. What was challenged was federal jurisdiction to control dumping in provincial waters of substances not shown to have a pollutant effect in extraprovincial waters. The trial judge and the Court of Appeal held the section to be *ultra vires* and dismissed the charges.

On appeal to the Supreme Court of Canada, a majority of the judges reviewed the national concern doctrine of the federal peace, order and good government power and drew the following conclusions:

1. The national concern doctrine is distinct from the national emergency doctrine of the peace, order and good government power;
2. The national concern doctrine applies to new matters arising since Confederation and to matters which have evolved from being of a local nature to being of national concern;
3. A matter of national concern must have a "singleness, distinctiveness and indivisibility" distinguishing it from matters of provincial concern; and
4. A relevant consideration in determining singleness, distinctiveness and indivisibility is the effect on extraprovincial interests of a provincial failure to deal effectively with the control or regulation of the intraprovincial aspects of the matter.

Marine pollution was held to be a matter of national concern because of its predominantly extraprovincial and international character. The degree of uncertainty in visually observing the boundary between the territorial sea and internal marine waters constituted an essential indivisibility of the matter of marine pollution by the dumping of substances. Dumping to pollute marine waters was held to be sufficiently distinguishable from dumping to pollute fresh water to meet the requirement of singleness or indivisibility. The Ocean Dumping Control Act distinguished between the pollution of salt water and the pollution of fresh water, therefore its impact on provincial jurisdiction had ascertainable and reasonable limits. As such, the matter qualified as one of national concern falling within the federal peace, order and good government power. The legislation was valid, the appeal was allowed, and the matter was referred back to the trial judge.

The dissenting judges would have dismissed the appeal, saying that the legislation encompassed activities falling within the exclusive jurisdiction of the province, and it could not be justified under the peace, order and good government power.

56. *Ontario Hydro v. Ontario (Labour Relations Board)*
[1993] 3 S.C.R. 327, 107 D.L.R. (4th) 457

A union applied under the Ontario Labour Relations Act to the respondent, OLRB, for certification as the exclusive bargaining agent for a unit of employees of the appellant, OH. Some of these employees worked at nuclear generating stations. Another group of employees challenged the application on the ground that those employees who worked at the nuclear plants were within the jurisdiction of the Canada Labour Code and the Canada Labour Relations Board.

OLRB held hearings and concluded that it did not have jurisdiction to certify the bargaining unit in the application because the employees of the nuclear stations fell within federal labour jurisdiction. OH applied to the Ontario Divisional Court for judicial review. The decision of OLRB was quashed and an order of *mandamus* issued. The Ontario Court of Appeal allowed the appeal and reinstated the decision of OLRB. An appeal was brought to the Supreme Court of Canada on the question of whether the Ontario Labour Relations Act or the Canada Labour Code applied to relations between OH and its employees of nuclear generating stations.

The appeal was dismissed. A majority of the Court observed that s. 92(10)(*c*) of the Constitution Act, 1867 authorized Parliament to declare local works to be for the general advantage of Canada. In this case, the federal Atomic Energy Control Act declared that all works and undertakings constructed for the production, use and application of atomic energy were for the general advantage of Canada. Legislative jurisdiction conferred over a declared work involved control over its operation and management, with a vital part of the power of management being the power to regulate labour relations. Furthermore, the production, use and application of atomic energy constituted a matter of national concern. This, together with its predominantly extraprovincial and international character made it subject to Parliament's power to legislate for the peace, order and good government of Canada.

The dissenting judges observed that the federal government exercised exclusive jurisdiction over some aspects of OH's nuclear plants through its declaratory power and its power to legislate for peace, order and good government. However, control of labour relations was not seen as integral to Parliament's effective regulation of the nuclear plants. Therefore, labour relations would have been under provincial jurisdiction.

Trade and Commerce

57. *Proprietary Articles Trade Association v. Attorney General for Canada*
[1931] 1 A.C. 310

The appellant, P, was found by a Commission appointed under the federal Combines Investigation Act to be party to a combine as defined in the Act. A reference was brought to the Supreme Court of Canada to determine the validity of the Combines Investigation Act, as well as the validity of s. 498 of the Criminal Code, which made it an offence to conspire to limit transportation facilities, to restrain commerce, to unduly lessen manufacturing or to unduly prevent competition. The Supreme Court of Canada held both pieces of legislation to be valid.

The Privy Council dismissed the appeal on the ground that the legislation fell within Parliament's criminal law power. Observing that "criminal law" meant "criminal law in its widest sense", the Court held that the power extended to legislation to make new crimes. The legislation in this case defined and made criminal those combines which were seen to be contrary to the public interest. It was not in substance an attempt to use criminal law power to justify an interference with provincial rights.

The Court therefore found it unnecessary to support the legislation under the federal power to regulate trade and commerce. However, their Lordships responded to an argument against the validity of the legislation on the basis of *In re The Board of Commerce Act, 1919 (46)*. They held that the decision could not be construed to say that the power to regulate trade and commerce could be invoked only in furtherance of a general power which Parliament possessed independently of it. Parliament had an independent authority over the particular subject matter, although the extent of that authority was not defined.

58. *The King v. Eastern Terminal Elevator Co.*
[1925] S.C.R. 434, [1925] 3 D.L.R. 1

Subsection 95(7) of the Canada Grain Act provided that if the amount of grain found in a terminal elevator at the end of a crop year exceeded a specified amount, the excess was to be sold and the proceeds paid to the Board of Grain Commissioners. The Crown brought an action against the respondent, E, under this provision, claiming the amount of the excess grain or its cash equivalent. The respondent denied the existence of a surplus and in the alternative contended that the provision and the entire Act were *ultra vires*. The Exchequer Court held the subsection to be *ultra vires* on the ground that in dealing with a right of ownership of grain, it was within the legislative competence of the provinces.

The Supreme Court of Canada dismissed the appeal. The purpose of the Canada Grain Act was to regulate the grain trade in Canada, both locally and in respect of interprovincial and external trade. The fact that a large part of the grain trade was external trade did not justify the regulation of local trade. The statute could not be sustained as being legislation in relation to agriculture, nor could it be upheld as being for the general advantage of Canada, or as addressing a national emergency.

In dissent, Anglin J. held that no single province could legislate to cover the quality control aspects of the scheme of the Act. Therefore, the subject matter of the Act was beyond the scope of provincial powers. In addition, the Act could have been supported under s. 91 of the British North America Act as being in relation to the regulation of trade and commerce.

59. *Reference re the Farm Products Marketing Act*
[1957] S.C.R. 198

A provision of the Ontario Farm Products Marketing Act empowered the Farm Products Marketing Board to authorize marketing agencies to operate marketing schemes for certain regulated farm products. A reference was brought to the Supreme Court of Canada to determine the validity of the provision. The question referred to the Court assumed that the Act applied only to "intra-provincial transactions".

The regulation of trade and commerce was distinguished from the regulation of sale and purchase agreements. The former was within the jurisdiction of Parliament, the latter within the jurisdiction of the provinces. Once an article of sale entered the flow of interprovincial or external trade, the subject matter of the sale was no longer a local concern. The difficulty in this case was establishing if the subject matter of the legislation involved the transition from merely local to interprovincial trade and commerce. On the facts, the legislation was seen to be a regulation of property and civil rights in the province, and was therefore *intra vires.*

60. *Murphy v. C.P.R. and Attorney General for Canada*
[1958] S.C.R. 626

The appellant, M, brought three sacks of grain, all grown in Manitoba, to the respondent, C, for carriage to British Columbia. C refused to take delivery on the ground that it was prohibited from doing so by s. 32 of the Canadian Wheat Board Act. That section prevented anyone other than the Canadian Wheat Board from transporting wheat or wheat products from one province to another, or from selling or buying such commodities between provinces. The appellant brought an action in damages against C. His action was dismissed at trial and on appeal.

It was alleged that the Canadian Wheat Board Act interfered with property and civil rights in the province. It was also alleged that s. 32 enabled the Wheat Board to exact a tax on grain transported between provinces, which was inconsistent with s. 121 of the British North America Act (the "BNA Act"). That section provided for free admittance into all provinces of all articles of growth, produce or manufacture of any of the provinces.

The Supreme Court of Canada upheld the Canadian Wheat Board Act as being in relation to the regulation of trade and commerce. It was therefore within the competence of Parliament to enact and so the fact that it interfered with property and civil rights in the province was immaterial to its validity. The purpose of s. 121 of the BNA Act was described as prohibiting the establishment of customs duties affecting interprovincial trade. Nothing in the Canadian Wheat Board Act was in conflict with this provision.

61. *The Queen v. Klassen*
(1959), 20 D.L.R. (2d) 406, 29 W.W.R. 369 (Man. C.A.)

The respondent, K, was convicted under s. 16 of the Canadian Wheat Board Act on a charge of failing to record in a permit book the delivery of a quantity of wheat that he had purchased. He appealed his conviction, alleging that s. 16 of the Act was *ultra vires*. He also challenged the validity of s. 45, which declared all flour mills, feed mills, feed warehouses and seed cleaning mills to be works for the general advantage of Canada. K was the operator of a feed mill.

The Manitoba Court of Appeal held that the principal purpose of the Act, being the regulation of interprovincial and export trade, was legislation in relation to the regulation of trade and commerce. Although the legislation did affect property and civil rights in the province, such interference was incidental or ancillary to the achievement of the provision of an export market, which was a matter of national importance. The fact that K operated his feed mill in a local and provincial manner without engaging in external or interprovincial trade was irrelevant to his conviction. Since the legislation was valid the conviction was upheld. The issue was determined without assessing the validity of s. 45.

62. *Carnation Co. Ltd. v. Quebec Agricultural Marketing Board*
[1968] S.C.R. 238

The respondent, Q, was created by the Quebec Agricultural Marketing Act. The Act provided that producers of agricultural products in the province could apply to Q for approval of joint marketing plans. In addition to approving the plans, Q could arbitrate disputes arising out of the execution of such plans. The appellant, C, was a company whose Quebec operations processed raw milk into evaporated milk, most of which was sold outside the province.

Q had approved a joint plan submitted by the Quebec Carnation Company Milk Producers' Plan. The order approving the plan set up a board which was allowed to negotiate on behalf of the milk producers for the sale of their products to C. When there was no agreement as to the purchase price, Q arbitrated the matter and in two separate orders set a price. C attacked the validity of Q's decisions on the ground that the legislation was an attempt to regulate trade and commerce. The decisions were upheld by the Superior Court and the Appeal Side of the Court of Queen's Bench.

C argued that the orders enabled Q to set a price for a product which, after processing, would mainly be used for export outside Quebec. As such it was regulation of trade and commerce and beyond the competence of the provincial Legislature. This argument was rejected by the Supreme Court of Canada. The price determined by the orders would have had an effect on C's export trade, but this did not necessarily constitute regulation of trade and commerce. The question was not whether the orders affected interprovincial trade, but whether they were made "in relation to" the regulation of trade and commerce. The orders did not purport to control or restrict trade, and there was no evidence that they did in fact control or restrict it. Therefore, the appeal was dismissed.

63. *Attorney General for Manitoba v. Manitoba Egg and Poultry Association*
[1971] S.C.R. 689, 19 D.L.R. (3d) 169

Ontario chicken producers faced competition from Quebec producers who were able to supply inexpensive chickens. Quebec egg producers faced competition from Ontario producers who supplied inexpensive eggs. Ontario and Quebec passed legislation to create marketing schemes to protect their chicken and egg producers, respectively. To protect the interests of its own producers from these schemes, the Province of Manitoba passed similar legislation and brought a reference to the Court of Appeal to determine its validity. The legislation consisted of a regulation and order creating a plan whose purpose was "to obtain for producers the most advantageous marketing conditions for the regulated product" and to "avoid overproduction thereof". The Manitoba Court of Appeal held the legislation to be invalid.

The Supreme Court of Canada dismissed the appeal. The plan devised under the legislation was intended to govern the sale of all eggs in Manitoba, regardless of where they were produced. It was to be operated by and for the benefit of Manitoba egg producers, and carried out by a Board that had the power to control or prohibit the sale in Manitoba of eggs brought in from outside the province. The plan was considered to not only affect interprovincial trade in eggs, but to regulate such trade. It was designed to limit the free flow of trade between provinces, and therefore it invaded the legislative authority of Parliament to regulate trade and commerce. The portions of the regulation and order dealing with local trade in eggs were considered not to be severable and so the entire plan was held to be invalid.

64.   *Caloil Inc. v. Attorney General for Canada*
[1971] S.C.R. 543, 20 D.L.R. (3d) 472

The appellant, C, was an importer and distributor of petroleum products. C had contracted for the delivery of a quantity of gasoline from Spain at about the same time that certain provisions of the National Energy Board Act and the National Energy Board Regulations were amended. The effect of the amendments was to make licences for the import of motor gasoline conditional on the importer selling or delivering the gasoline to a defined geographic region. C did not comply with the conditions of licences issued under the amended Regulations and was refused a further licence. C applied to the Exchequer Court for a declaration that the regulatory scheme brought about by the amendments was unconstitutional.

The Exchequer Court declared the legislative scheme invalid and held that C was entitled to import motor gasoline without any restriction on its marketing after import. The Regulations were amended and under the amended scheme the National Energy Board refused licences for import without a declaration that the gasoline would be consumed where it was imported. A second action was brought in the Exchequer Court for declaratory relief. The Court dismissed the action and an appeal was taken to the Supreme Court of Canada.

The Supreme Court interpreted the amended Regulations as demonstrating a policy of controlling imports to foster the development and utilization of Canadian oil resources. The market for imported gasoline was restricted in order to reserve the market in other areas for domestic products. Therefore, the true character of the enactment was the administration of an extraprovincial marketing scheme. The interference with local trade was an integral part of the extraprovincial trade policy and so did not improperly invade provincial jurisdiction. The former Regulations did not purport to regulate "imported goods", because they applied to "any motor gasoline", so the first decision of the Exchequer Court was not *res judicata*.

65.   *Burns Foods Ltd. v. Attorney General of Manitoba*
[1975] 1 S.C.R. 494, 40 D.L.R. (3d) 731

Manitoba Regulation 180/71 established the Manitoba Hog Producers Marketing Plan, which defined "producer" as one who kept or slaughtered hogs within the province. Man. Reg. 4/72 prohibited purchase of hogs from a producer except where the purchase was made through the Hog Producers Marketing Board (the "Board"). Man. Reg. 97/72 prohibited slaughter of hogs in Manitoba unless the hogs were purchased from the Board. Hogs brought into the province were deemed to have been produced in Manitoba and were subject to the Act and Regulations as though they had actually been produced in Manitoba.

The Board brought an application for an injunction against the appellant, B, and other meat packers to restrain them from slaughtering hogs not purchased from the Board. The injunction was granted and affirmed on appeal. B counterclaimed for a declaration that The Natural Products Marketing Act and Regulations were *ultra vires* the province.

In the Supreme Court of Canada, a majority of the Court interpreted the effect of Man. Reg. 97/72 to be that B was prohibited from slaughtering in Manitoba hogs raised in any other province, unless the hogs were purchased from the producer through the Board. As such, if B were to purchase hogs in, for example, Saskatchewan from Saskatchewan producers, the contract would be governed by the Manitoba Regulations. This was beyond the competence of the Provincial Legislature, and it could not be considered to be an accessory of the local trade.

The Crown argued that Man. Reg. 97/72 applied only to hogs brought within the province and was therefore valid. This argument was rejected on the ground that there was a prescription for the conditions under which hogs could be brought in, which was in itself interprovincial trade. Subjecting sales of imported hogs to the same regulations as local sales was also regulation of interprovincial trade. The appeal was allowed, the injunction dissolved, the action dismissed, and the counterclaim allowed to the extent of declaring Man. Reg. 97/72 null and void.

Ritchie J. dissented, agreeing with the Court of Appeal that the legislation was primarily directed to the slaughter of hogs within a province and that it was a scheme to control local trade which merely incidentally affected interprovincial trade.

66.   *MacDonald v. Vapor Canada Ltd.*
[1977] 2 S.C.R. 134, 66 D.L.R. (3d) 1

The appellant, M, was an employee of the respondent, V. When he was hired he signed an agreement preventing him from disclosing to unauthorized persons any confidential information obtained in the course of his employment. After he left V he used information obtained from his employment in submitting a tender to secure a contract for which V had also submitted a tender. V brought an action in the Federal Court for damages, and obtained an interlocutory injunction restraining M from using in his business any confidential information acquired through his employment with V.

On appeal, a constitutional issue was raised as to the jurisdiction of the Federal Court, which in turn was based on the validity of ss. 7, 53 and 55 of the Trade Marks Act. Section 7 of the Act prohibited such things as making false statements to discredit competitors, passing off, and misleading the public as to wares for sale. In particular, subs. 7(*e*) prohibited any act or business practice contrary to honest industrial or commercial usage in Canada. Section 53 provided for a court of competent jurisdiction to grant relief by way of injuction or damages for any breach of the provisions of the Act. Section 55 granted jurisdiction to the Federal

Court to hear proceedings brought to enforce provisions of the Act. The Federal Court of Appeal upheld the interlocutory injunction.

The Supreme Court of Canada rejected the argument that subs. 7(*e*) was in relation to trade and commerce. The provision was directed to the ethical conduct of persons engaged in business, and as such would be invalid unless it were part of a larger regulatory scheme governing trading relations of more than a local concern. Section 7 in general merely overlaid or extended known civil causes of action reflecting issues falling within provincial legislative competence. Parliament could not create a statutory cause of action for the breach of contract, breach of confidence, and misappropriation of confidential information that was the subject matter of this case.

The Court also rejected arguments that the legislation could be supported under criminal law power or under federal treaty implementing power. The appeal was allowed.

67. *Re Agricultural Products Marketing Act*
[1978] 2 S.C.R. 1198, 84 D.L.R. (3d) 257

The federal Minister of Agriculture and the provinces entered into an agreement to develop a comprehensive national egg marketing scheme, regulating the marketing of eggs in intraprovincial, interprovincial and export trade. Following this agreement the Executive Council of Ontario referred 13 questions to the Ontario Court of Appeal concerning the validity of certain provisions of three statutes, and related orders and regulations. The three statutes were the federal Agricultural Products Marketing Act, the federal Farm Products Marketing Agencies Act, and the provincial Farm Products Marketing Act.

Those attacking the legislation alleged that the federal statutes encroached upon provincial jurisdiction in relation to local or intraprovincial trade, and that the provincial statutes reached into federal jurisdiction over interprovincial and export trade. An appeal was brought to the Supreme Court of Canada on 10 questions, some of which dealt with specific orders made under the legislation.

One of the questions asked whether ss. 2 and 3 of the federal Agricultural Products Marketing Act were *ultra vires*. Those sections dealt with delegation and levies relating to interprovincial and export trade, and were *intra vires*. The exception was subs. 2(2)(*a*), which was invalid because it dealt with adjustment levies, a matter within provincial jurisdiction.

The Farm Products Marketing Agencies Act, which concerned the functions of federal marketing agencies relating to intraprovincial trade, was seen by the majority to be an enactment for proper federal purposes, rather than a federal intrusion into local trade.

A regulation under the Ontario Farm Products Marketing Act provided for quotas for egg producers. On the issue of the validity of these provisions, control of production was seen to be a local matter, whether the production was agricultural or industrial. The egg farms were local undertakings subject to provincial authority, regardless of where the eggs were ultimately sold. The legislation was not aimed at controlling interprovincial trade, but rather complementary to federal regulations. It was therefore valid as being within provincial jurisdiction.

68. *Attorney General for Canada v. Canadian National Transportation Ltd.*
[1983] 2 S.C.R. 206, 3 D.L.R. (4th) 16

The respondent, C, was charged with unlawful conspiracy to prevent or lessen competition in interprovincial transportation, under subs.32(1)(c) of the federal Combines Investigation Act. Pursuant to the Act, conduct of the proceedings against the respondent was assigned to the appellant, AG, who brought an information before the Alberta Provincial Court. The respondent sought an order of prohibition to restrain that court from hearing the matter. It was argued that under subs. 92(14) of the British North America Act, the provinces were responsible for the administration of criminal justice in the province. Since subs. 32(1)(c) was criminal law, only a provincial Attorney General could conduct prosecutions.

The trial judge dismissed the application for prohibition. The Alberta Court of Appeal reversed this decision, holding subs. 32(1)(c) to be criminal law legislation and not legislation in relation to trade and commerce. Therefore, the prosecution should have been conducted by a provincial Attorney General. There was an appeal to the Supreme Court of Canada on two questions: (1) Does subs. 32(1)(c) depend on the federal criminal law power for its validity? (2) If so, can the Attorney General for Canada be authorized to conduct criminal proceedings pursuant to that section?

Laskin C.J. speaking for a majority of the Court considered that there was no distinction between offences resting on a violation of trade and commerce legislation and those resting on a violation of criminal law. Subsection 92(14) did not specifically mention criminal offences, so if the provinces controlled criminal prosecutions, they would also control prosecutions for violation of legislation other than criminal law. However, he based his reasons on the assumption that the Act rested only on criminal law power. Subsection 92(14) granted jurisdiction over the administration of justice, including the constitution, maintenance and organization of criminal courts. However, there was no granting of jurisdiction over the conduct of criminal prosecutions. The administration of "justice in the province" was interpreted as dealing with the operation of judicial machinery within the province, not with the matter of who should enforce and prosecute breaches of federal statutes. At the least, Parliament had concurrent jurisdiction with the provinces to enforce federal legislation validly enacted under criminal law power.

Dickson J. held that it was necessary to determine whether and how far the impugned legislation encroached on provincial autonomy in the regulation of trade. A federal enactment could not regulate a single trade or business in the province by purporting to create a uniform regulation across all the provinces. However, federal legislation could validly address the economy as a single national unit rather then as a collection of individual local enterprises. In this case, subs. 32(1)(*c*) was viewed not as an isolated provision, but rather as part of a regulatory scheme. A scheme aimed at the regulation of competition could not practically or constitutionally be enacted by a provincial government, given the vast scope of interprovincial trade. The federal trade and commerce power complemented, rather than eroded, provincial autonomy. Therefore, subs. 32(1)(*c*) was held to be valid under the federal trade and commerce power. The provision could also be supported under the federal criminal law power. As a result, there was concurrent federal and provincial prosecutorial authority.

The questions were answered in the affirmative, and the appeal was allowed.

69. *General Motors of Canada Limited v. City National Leasing*
[1989] 1 S.C.R. 641, 58 D.L.R. (4th) 255

The respondent, C, was in the business of leasing fleets of automobiles and trucks. Most of its vehicles were purchased from the appellant, G. C alleged that G had been granting a preferential interest rate on vehicles sold to competitors of C. C asserted that this was a practice of price discrimination contrary to the Combines Investigation Act. Section 31.1 of the Act created a civil cause of action for certain breaches of the Act. C brought an action against G under the section for the amount of interest it had paid in excess of the amount paid by its competitors.

G brought an application before a motions court judge to strike certain paragraphs of the statement of claim as disclosing no cause of action. G alleged that s. 31.1 was in pith and substance legislation in relation to matters of property and civil rights in the province and matters of a local nature, and therefore *ultra vires*.

The motions court judge on other grounds held that there was no cause of action, but the decision was reversed by the Court of Appeal, who affirmed the validity of s. 31.1.

The Supreme Court of Canada adopted a three-step approach in assessing the validity of the legislation. The first step was to determine whether the impugned provision intruded on provincial power and if so, to what extent. Section 31.1 created a civil right of action which *prima facie* invaded provincial power. However it was not a significant intrusion because the provision was remedial, its application was limited by the other provisions of the Act, and federal encroachment in the matter of civil causes of action was not unprecedented.

The second step was to determine whether the Act contained a regulatory scheme. The Combines Investigation Act identified and defined anticompetitive conduct, created an investigatory procedure, and established criminal and administrative remedies against companies engaging in prohibited behaviour. These factors were taken as evidence of a scheme of regulation designed to discourage forms of commercial behaviour detrimental to the Canadian economy. It was found that effective regulation of competition law required national regulation, therefore the scheme was held to be valid as legislation in relation to general trade and commerce.

The third step involved an assessment of whether the impugned provision could be upheld by being sufficiently integrated with the valid scheme. The fact that a provision was merely included in a valid scheme would be insufficient. By the fact that s. 31.1 reinforced other sanctions of the Act, was bounded by the parameters of the Act, and was fundamentally integrated into the purpose and underlying philosophy of the Act, it was held to be "functionally related" to the Act as a whole and was therefore valid. The appeal was dismissed.

See also *A.G. British Columbia v. A.G. Canada (The Natural Products Marketing Act) (49)*

Federal and Provincial Taxation

70. *Bank of Toronto v. Lambe*
(1887), 12 App. Cas. 575 (P.C.)

The appellant, B, had its head office in Toronto but also carried on business in Montreal. The respondent, L, represented the Government of Quebec. The Quebec Provincial Legislature passed a statute which imposed a tax on several types of businesses. For banks, the amount of tax was calculated on their paid-up capital, plus an additional amount for each place of business. B refused to pay, alleging that the tax was invalid because the statute was beyond the competence of the Provincial Legislature. L brought an action to recover the amount of tax due.

The Superior Court of Quebec dismissed the action on the grounds that the tax was indirect, that it was not imposed within the limits of the province, and that regulation of banks was a matter for Parliament. The Court of Queen's Bench allowed the appeal on the grounds that the tax was direct, and that it was a matter of a local or private nature in the province.

On appeal, the Privy Council considered whether the tax was direct so as to bring it within class 2 of s. 92 of the British North America Act. If so, it would be within the power of the provinces, and thus it would be necessary to establish whether anything in s. 91 brought the tax in question out of provincial jurisdiction.

The Court concluded that the tax was direct, on the basis of the definition by John Stuart Mill:

> A direct tax is one which is demanded from the very persons who it is intended or desired should pay it. Indirect taxes are those which are demanded from one person in the expectation and intention that he shall indemnify himself at the expense of another; such are the excise or customs.
>
> (*Political Economy*, ed. 1886, vol. ii., p. 415)

In this case the tax was found to be demanded directly from the bank to raise money for provincial purposes. It was not a tax on commodities, profits, or transactions. It was direct payment of a lump sum. The Court went on to say:

> It may possibly happen that in the intricacies of mercantile dealings the bank may find a way to recoup itself out of the pockets of its Quebec customers. But the way must be an obscure and circuitous one, the amount of recoupment cannot bear any direct relation to the amount of tax paid, and if the bank does manage it, the result will not improbably disappoint the intention and desire of the Quebec Government.
>
> (Whyte, Lederman & Bur, p. 9-47–48)

As such the tax was held to be a direct one. The tax was taxation within the province even though B had its domicile and capital in Toronto, because class 2 of s. 92 did not contemplate a domicile or residence requirement. B carried on business in Quebec and on that basis was directly taxed by the province.

The Court followed *Citizens Insurance Company v. Parsons (7)* to hold that general taxing power of Parliament should not override the particular provincial taxing power. Direct taxation within the province to raise revenue for provincial purposes was a subject falling wholly within the jurisdiction of the provinces. The appeal was dismissed.

71.   *Caron v. The King*
[1924] A.C. 999 (P.C.)

The appellant, C, was the Minister of Agriculture of the Province of Quebec. Under the federal Income War Tax Act, he was taxed on his salary as Minister and on his sessional indemnity as a member of the Legislature. C contended that he was not liable to pay the tax on the grounds that the legislation was *ultra vires* and that in any event his income was not taxable.

The Exchequer Court ordered C to pay the tax plus interest and costs, and the decision was affirmed by the Supreme Court of Canada.

The Privy Council reviewed ss. 91(3) and 92(2) of the British North America Act, setting out the powers of taxation of Parliament and of the Provincial Legislatures, respectively. It was held that the two sections were to be construed together. Section 91(3) granted to the Dominion the power to impose taxation for Dominion purposes. Nothing in s. 92(2), allowing for direct taxation within the province to raise revenue for provincial purposes, derogated from that power. Therefore, the Act was *intra vires*. Furthermore, there was no reason why any sources of C's income should be removed from Parliament's power of taxation. The appeal was dismissed.

72. *City of Halifax v. Fairbanks*
[1928] A.C. 117 (P.C.)

The respondent, F, owned property in the City of Halifax which it leased to the federal Crown for use as a ticket office of Canadian National Railways. The lease provided that the lessee should pay the business taxes on the premises. F was assessed business taxes by the appellant, H, in respect of the property, but the assessment was appealed on the basis that the tax was void as not being direct taxation within the province. The assessment was upheld by the Supreme Court of Nova Scotia, but the decision was reversed by a majority of the Supreme Court of Canada.

In the Privy Council F argued that the occupation by the Crown could not be held to be for gain and as such the property was not subject to business tax. This argument was rejected. It was also argued that the tax was on property belonging to Canada and was therefore void. However, tax on property leased to the federal Crown was considered not to be tax on the property of Canada, so this argument also failed.

On the issue of whether the tax was direct, the Privy Council disagreed with the reasoning of the Supreme Court of Canada. The Supreme Court held that it was reasonable to expect that F would exact indemnity from the Crown for the tax, given that the tax was imposed in respect of the purposes for which the property was leased. Therefore, the tax was indirect and beyond the jurisdiction of the provinces. However, the Privy Council considered the true question to be not one of who ultimately bears the tax, but rather whether the tax is in its nature a direct one under the meaning of class 2 of s. 92 of the British North America Act.

Death duties, municipal and local rates, and taxes imposed on property and income were held to be direct taxation, "according to the common understanding of the term" (Whyte, Lederman & Bur, p. 9-58). The tax in this case was a tax on property and held to be direct taxation. The appeal was allowed and the decision of the Supreme Court of Nova Scotia restored.

73. *The King v. Caledonian Collieries*
[1928] A.C. 358 (P.C.)

The Alberta Legislature passed an act which imposed a tax on all mine owners. The tax was calculated as not more than two per cent of the gross revenue of the mine and was to be remitted monthly. The respondent, C, was a company which owned mines as defined by the provincial legislation. When the company refused to pay the tax, the Crown brought an action to recover the amounts due.

The Chief Justice of Alberta held the Act to be *intra vires*, a decision which was affirmed by a majority of the Appellate Division of the Alberta Supreme Court. The Supreme Court of Canada held the tax to be indirect and therefore the legislation was *ultra vires*.

The Privy Council looked at the real nature of the tax to determine whether or not it was direct taxation within the province within the meaning of s. 92 of the British North America Act. Although the tax was said to be imposed on "gross revenue", it was found to be indistinguishable from a tax upon receipts from all sales. The Court observed that the "general tendency" of the tax would be such that the company would try to recover it in the purchase price. Therefore the tax was indirect and thus invalid. It made no difference that the tax was not payable at the time a sale was made, since it was simple enough to anticipate the amount of the tax payable and add it to the purchase price. The appeal was dismissed.

74. *Attorney General for Canada v. Attorney General for Ontario*
(Unemployment Insurance)
[1937] A.C. 355 (P.C.)

Parliament passed the Unemployment and Social Insurance Act, 1935, which created a system of unemployment insurance. The system was funded by Parliament and by mandatory contributions from both employers and employees. A reference was brought to the Supreme Court of Canada to determine the validity of the Act. A majority of the Court held that it was *ultra vires*.

The Privy Council observed that insurance of this kind, especially as it related to employment contracts, was *prima facie* within the competence of the provinces as being in relation to property and civil rights. It was argued that, under the circumstances, unemployment insurance was especially important to Canada. However, the Court found that the legislation was not enacted to deal with any special emergency, and it was intended to be permanent.

A second argument contended that the obligation on employers and employees to make contributions was a system of taxation. The money raised became public property, which was to be distributed according to the provisions of the Act. The legislation would thus be supported by Parliament's power to raise money by a system of taxation. The Privy Council observed that even assuming the existence of a system of taxation, Dominion legislation dealing with Dominion property could still be framed so as to invade provincial jurisdiction, and thus be *ultra vires*. In this case, the legislation was held to be in pith and substance an insurance act affecting the civil rights of employers and employees in each province. The Act was therefore *ultra vires*, and the appeal from the Supreme Court was dismissed.

75.   *Atlantic Smoke Shops Ltd. v. Conlon*
       [1943] A.C. 550 (P.C.)

The legislature of New Brunswick enacted the Tobacco Tax Act, 1940. The Act provided for the payment of tax on tobacco purchased for private consumption from a retail vendor. Where the purchase was made by an agent on behalf of a principal, the tax was payable by the agent. If a resident of New Brunswick were to bring tobacco into the province for private consumption, the tax liability would be the same as if the tobacco had been purchased through a retail vendor in the province.

A stated case was submitted to the Supreme Court of New Brunswick, Appeal Division, which upheld the validity of the legislation. On appeal, a majority of the Supreme Court of Canada held that the Act was valid, except for the provisions imposing tax liability on an agent.

The Privy Council held that the tax imposed on a purchaser for private consumption in the province was a direct tax because it was paid by the last purchaser, with no question of resale, and no opportunity to pass the tax on to another. It was argued that the tax was in the nature of excise and thus beyond the legislative competence of the province. However, the Court found it unnecessary to consider this issue in light of the finding that the tax was clearly direct and therefore within provincial jurisdiction.

With respect to purchases by an agent, the Privy Council held that the tax was actually borne by the principal, even though paid by the agent. Indemnification of the agent by the principal for the tax paid was not made pursuant to any fresh transaction in the nature of a resale; the payment of the tax was rather seen as part of a single transaction. The fact that the tax was paid by the principal through the agent did not create a sufficient distinction to characterize the tax as indirect.

The provisions for payment of tax on tobacco brought into the province were challenged on the ground that they restricted the free flow of goods between provinces, contrary to s. 121 of the British North America Act. However, the tax was considered not to be a customs duty restricting the flow of goods, it was a direct tax exacted from persons within the province.

The Act was therefore upheld in its entirety as legislation in relation to direct taxation within the province. The decision of the Supreme Court was varied to the extent that it held the tax imposed on agents to be invalid.

76. *Texada Mines Ltd. v. Attorney General of British Columbia*
[1960] S.C.R. 713, 24 D.L.R. (2d) 81

The Mineral Property Taxation Act of British Columbia provided that, for lands containing mineral deposits, the owners of such lands were subject to a tax based on the value of the minerals. Regulations made pursuant to the Act set the tax rate at eight per cent for 1958. The provincial Iron Bounty Act permitted the Crown to pay a bounty to iron producers for each ton of iron processed from ore smelted within the province.

The appellant, T, owned lands and mineral claims in British Columbia, and carried on the business of mining iron ore. The ore was sold overseas. It was not processed within the province for lack of an available smelter. Therefore, T was unable to make any claims under the Iron Bounty Act.

The validity of the Mineral Property Taxation Act was challenged on the ground that it imposed an indirect tax. T contended that the purpose of the Act was to impose a tax on iron ore sold for export, and that the tax was assessed on the ore rather than the land, such that it would be added to the ultimate sale price.

The trial judge held the Act to be *ultra vires*. The Court of Appeal held the Act to be valid, with the exception of regulations prescribing the method of assessment, which were found to be in conflict with and beyond the powers conferred by the Act.

The Supreme Court of Canada found that the rate of tax imposed on iron ore was inordinately high in relation to other metals mined in the province, and that T could not profitably operate its business if it were subject to the proposed rate. This led to the conclusion that the true nature and purpose of the legislation was not to raise revenue for provincial purposes, but to impede the export of iron ore in order to encourage manufacturing activities. The tax was therefore an export tax which was indirect, and *ultra vires* the provincial Legislature. The appeal was allowed.

77. *Canadian Industrial Gas & Oil Ltd. v. The Government of Saskatchewan*
[1978] 2 S.C.R. 545, 80 D.L.R. (3d) 449

Following the sharp rise in world oil prices in 1973, the Government of Saskatchewan enacted legislation imposing a mineral tax and royalty surcharge on income received from oil produced in Saskatchewan. The tax was the full amount of the difference between the amount actually received at the well-head and the basic well-head price, a figure fixed by statute. The effect was that the Government of Saskatchewan would acquire the benefit of all increases in the value of Saskatchewan oil above the basic well-head price. Almost all of that oil was exported.

The appellant, C, was an oil producer. C challenged the validity of the legislation on the grounds that the mineral tax and the royalty surcharge constituted indirect taxation, and that the legislation regulated interprovincial and international trade and commerce. Both the trial judge and the Court of Appeal upheld the validity of the legislation.

In the Supreme Court of Canada, the royalty surcharge was held not to be a true royalty, but rather a levy on production, and as such was a tax in the same nature as the mineral tax. The mineral tax, though it was called a "mineral income tax", was held not to be an income tax in any generally recognized sense of the term. Therefore, the contention that the tax was direct as being an income tax was rejected.

The real substance and intent of the legislation was that the mineral tax and the royalty surcharge were taxes on oil production. Virtually all of the oil produced was destined for export. The tax was thus an export tax, and therefore indirect. The legislation purported to impose a direct tax on the producer which could not be passed on to the purchaser. However, the true effect of the legislation was to restrict the producer to retaining no more than the basic well-head price. Any amount in excess paid by the purchaser would be recovered by the Government by way of the tax. The purchaser paid the tax as part of the purchase price, so the tax was not direct and therefore *ultra vires* the province.

The legislation allowed the province to fix the price of oil, which had almost no market within the province. Therefore, the legislation was *ultra vires* as being in relation to the regulation of interprovincial trade.

Dickson J. in dissent held that the true nature and effect of the legislation was direct taxation within the province for the purpose of raising revenue for provincial purposes, and that it was not merely a colourable device for assuming control of interprovincial trade.

78. *The Queen in the Right of Manitoba v. Air Canada*
[1980] 2 S.C.R. 303, 111 D.L.R. (3d) 513

The Province of Manitoba assessed the respondent, A, for taxes for operations and services under the provincial Retail Sales Tax Act. The tax was imposed for flights landing and taking off in the province, and for flights which did not touch down but passed through air space over the province. A successfully appealed the assessment to a judge of the Queen's Bench, and the Court of Appeal affirmed that there was no tax liability.

An appeal was taken to the Supreme Court of Canada on the issue of liability for tax in respect of liquor service on flights landing in Manitoba from outside the province, and on flights passing through provincial air space. The questions on appeal were whether the air space over the province was "within the province" so as to permit application of the Retail Sales Tax Act, and whether the Act was otherwise *intra vires*.

The Supreme Court assumed that the province had some legislative jurisdiction over its air space, but held that the action of passing through the air space did not give an aircraft a *situs* in the province. In order to support a tax "within the province", there had to be a substantial, as opposed to nominal, presence in the province. Flights landing in Manitoba were seen to have the same "momentary transitory presence", so the same reasoning applied. Therefore, the tax was held not to be "within the province" as contemplated by s. 92(2) of the British North America Act. The issue of whether or not the tax was direct was not addressed, and the appeal was dismissed.

79. *Winterhaven Stables Ltd. v. Canada (Attorney General)*
(1988), 53 D.L.R. (4th) 413, [1989] 1 W.W.R. 193 (Alta. C.A.)

The plaintiff, W, brought an action for a declaration that the Income Tax Act and certain federal spending statutes were *ultra vires* the Parliament of Canada. W alleged that the Income Tax Act constituted direct taxation within a province, and that the revenues raised by such direct taxation were for provincial purposes. The revenues funded programmes administered under the following statutes: the Federal-Provincial Fiscal Arrangements and Federal Post-Secondary Education and Health Contributions Act, the Canada Assistance Plan Act, the Canada Health Act, the Medical Care Act, the Hospital Insurance and Diagnostic Services Act, the Blind Persons Act, and the Disabled Persons Act. W contended that the Income Tax Act in conjunction with the conditional spending authorization contained in the other statutes constituted a scheme to regulate and indirectly legislate within areas of provincial jurisdiction. The action was dismissed by the trial judge.

The Court of Appeal agreed with the trial judge's holding that the Income Tax Act was not direct taxation within the province. Revenues raised under the Act became part of a Consolidated Revenue Fund, a nonsegregated fund used by Parliament to fund provincial programmes. Because there was no segregation there was no nexus between revenue from a specific source and expenditures paid from the Fund. The fact that the money raised by Parliament could have been used for purposes falling within the legislative jurisdiction of the provinces was not objectionable, because spending power was not the same as legislative power.

With respect to the spending statutes, the court observed that there was considerable pressure on the provinces to pass complementary legislation or otherwise comply with the conditions imposed on the allocated payments. However, the issues were not to be determined by considering the ultimate probable effect of the legislation. Parliament was entitled to legislate in relation to its own debt and its own property. It was further entitled to choose the means of spending the money raised through the exercise of its valid taxing power. By paying the money to the provinces it could impose conditions, as long as the conditions did not amount to a colourable scheme to control a matter outside federal authority. In this case there was no attempt to control or regulate the provincial use of the payments. Therefore, the spending statues were held to be *intra vires*, and the appeal was dismissed.

80.   *Reference re Canada Assistance Plan (British Columbia) (Constitutional Question Act)*
[1991] 2 S.C.R. 525, 127 N.R. 161

The Canada Assistance Plan (the "Plan") authorized the Government of Canada to enter into agreements with the provincial governments to pay them contributions toward their expenditures on social assistance and welfare. The Plan specified certain prerequisites for eligibility of expenditures, but the provinces were left to decide which programmes would receive money and to determine the level of spending. Agreements under the Plan were to continue in force as long as the relevant provincial law remained in operation, but could be terminated or amended by consent.

Parliament enacted the Government Expenditures Restraint Act, which was an attempt to reduce the federal budget deficit. The Act limited the growth of payments made to certain provinces under the Plan. One of the provinces affected was British Columbia. As a consequence, the Government of the province referred two questions to the British Columbia Court of Appeal: (1) Did the Government of Canada have any statutory, prerogative or contractual authority to limit its obligation under the Plan and its agreement with the Province of British Columbia? (2) Did the terms of the agreement, the conduct of the Government of Canada, and the provisions of the Plan give rise to a legitimate expectation that the Government of Canada would not attempt to limit its obligation under the agreement or the Plan without provincial consent?

A majority of the Court of Appeal held that there was no authority to limit the obligation, and that there was a legitimate expectation of consent to any changes.

The Supreme Court of Canada answered the first question in the affirmative. The contribution formula was not found in the agreement. The contribution formula was found in the Plan, which was subject to amendment. The agreement obliged the Government of Canada to pay to British Columbia contributions which were authorized from time to time under the Plan. The contributions were not restricted to payments authorized at the time the agreement was signed.

The second question was answered in the negative. If the doctrine of legitimate expectations could prevent the government from introducing legislation, the business of government would be paralyzed. Although the question was answered on this point, Sopinka J. addressed several other submissions. It was held that the question did not raise issues of constitutional convention or manner and form.

It was further argued that the proposed change to the Plan was *ultra vires* Parliament, because the legislation amounted to regulation of a matter outside federal authority. However, it was held that the simple withholding of federal money which had been granted to fund a matter within provincial jurisdiction did not amount to regulation of that matter.

Incorporation of Companies

81. *In re the Incorporation of Companies in Canada*
(1913), 48 S.C.R. 331

Under s. 92(11) of the British North America Act, the provinces were given the power to legislate for "the incorporation of companies with provincial objects". A series of questions were referred to the Supreme Court of Canada to interpret that section.

Of a six-member panel, two judges held that the words "provincial objects" referred to both a territorial limitation and a limitation on the character of the powers conferred on provincially incorporated companies. The creation of a company with capacity to carry on its business in more than one province was within the exclusive authority of Parliament. However, a provincially incorporated company could contract with nonresidents in matters ancillary to the exercise of the company's substantive powers.

Three judges held that "provincial objects" placed a limitation on the character of the powers only, and not on the territory. That is, a provincial legislature could not incorporate a company with Dominion objects. However, nothing in s. 92(11) precluded a provincially incorporated company from availing itself of the comity of another province or a foreign state. Therefore, a provincial company could operate in another province or foreign state as long as the other province or state recognized the company's existence and permitted its operation.

The sixth judge, Duff J., held that a province could confer upon its companies a capacity to acquire rights and exercise powers outside the province, as long as the business as a whole could be considered provincial, as opposed to extraprovincial. That issue was to be determined according to the circumstances of each case.

82. *Bonanza Creek Gold Mining Co. Ltd. v. The King*
[1916] 1 A.C. 566 (P.C.)

The appellant, B, was incorporated by letters patent under the authority of the Companies Act (Ontario) to carry on the business of mining. Nothing in the letters patent restricted the area of the company's operations. B, as assignees of leases granted by the Crown through the Minister of the Interior for Canada, operated hydraulic mining properties in Yukon Territory. The Minister also granted to B a free miner's certificate. It was alleged that certain mining claims had reverted to the Crown when the claims should have been leased to B under the terms of the lease agreements. Because of this and other alleged breaches of the agreements B presented a petition of right in the Exchequer Court to recover damages.

The Exchequer Court judge dismissed the petition of right on the ground that B had no power to operate a mining business outside its province of incorporation. The Supreme Court of Canada dismissed the appeal.

The Privy Council held that the free miner's certificate was validly issued. B therefore obtained a good title to the mining locations and had a licence to carry on business in Yukon, subject to the general question of whether a provincially incorporated company had the capacity to acquire and exercise rights outside the territorial boundaries of the province.

In answering the general question, the Court held that the character of the actual powers and rights the province could bestow to provincially incorporated companies was confined to powers and rights exercisable within the province. A distinction was then drawn between powers and rights and the capacity to accept powers and rights. A company created by charter had the capacity of a natural person to acquire powers and rights. In this case B was created by letters patent with no restriction on its capacity to accept powers and rights conferred by outside authorities. Therefore, B had the capacity to accept the rights conferred by the valid miner's certificate and the leases. The appeal was allowed, and it was ordered that there be a trial of the petition of right.

Transportation and Communication

83. *Toronto v. Bell Telephone*
[1905] A.C. 52 (P.C.)

The respondent, B, was incorporated under a Dominion statute for the purpose of carrying on the business of a national telephone company. A dispute soon arose in the province of Quebec as to B's capacity to carry on local business. As a consequence of this dispute B applied to the Ontario Legislature for authorization to exercise its powers within Ontario. The authorization included a condition that, in order to exercise its powers, B required the consent of the appropriate municipal council. When B attempted to construct lines in the city of Toronto, the appellant T brought proceedings for an injunction on the ground that B had failed to obtain the necessary consent.

The trial judge held that although the Act under which B was incorporated contemplated an interprovincial connection of B's business enterprise, no such connection actually existed. Therefore B could not exercise its powers without provincial authority and the action succeeded. However, the decision was reversed by the Court of Appeal, who said that "the failure or neglect to put into effect all the powers given by the legislative authority affords no ground for questioning the original jurisdiction."

The Privy Council observed that the scope of B's business was not confined to any one province. According to the British NorthAmerica Act, 1867, although the province had been given jurisdiction over "local works and undertakings", Parliament had jurisdiction over "works and undertakings connecting the province with any other". The Court agreed with the Court of Appeal, saying that it was not competent for a provincial legislature to limit or interfere with powers conferred by Parliament. B was not estopped from exercising its powers as a consequence of the condition of municipal consent. It made no difference that B carried on a local business and a long-distance business, for under the Act these two businesses were simply two components of a single undertaking. T's appeal was dismissed.

84. *Montreal v. Montreal Street Railway*
[1912] A.C. 333 (P.C.)

The Montreal Park and Island Railway ("Park Railway") and the respondent, MSR, were two railways operated in the city of Montreal. The two systems connected with each other at several points and the cars of each ran on the lines of the other. The Park Railway was created under provincial legislation, however it was later declared to be a work for the general advantage of Canada such that jurisdiction over it was withdrawn from the province and passed to Parliament.

A complaint about the Park Railway was brought to the federal Board of the Railway Commissioners (the "Board"). It was alleged that there was discrimination of services and rates as between a ward within the city and an outlying township. The Board found the discrimination to exist, and issued an order equalizing the services and rates. The order included a provision for MSR to enter into any agreements necessary to allow the Park Railway to comply with the terms of the order. The order was appealed to the Supreme Court of Canada on the ground that the Board had no jurisdiction over the provincial MSR. The appeal was allowed and the order set aside.

The Privy Council observed that the jurisdiction of the Board depended on the validity of s. 8 of the federal Railway Act. The section declared that any provincial railway connecting with or crossing any federal railway would be subject to the provisions of the Railway Act relating to line connections, through traffic, criminal matters, and navigable waters.

The Court stated that provincial rail companies could be expected to cooperate with federal rail companies, and provincial legislatures could be expected to exercise their legislative powers to enforce cooperative ventures between provincial and federal rail companies. Therefore, s. 8 could not be upheld as being necessarily incidental to Parliament's exercise of control over the traffic of a federal railway. Consequently, provincial railways could not by federal legislation be coerced into the types of agreements sought to be enforced in the order of the Board. Section 8 of the Railway Act was held to be *ultra vires*, the order affecting MSR was held to have been made without jurisdiction, and the appeal from the Supreme Court of Canada was dismissed.

85. *Re Regulation and Control of Aeronautics*
  [1932] A.C. 54 (P.C.)

After World War I the Supreme Council of the peace conference in Paris drew up a convention relating to the regulation of aerial navigation. To enable the performance of Canadian obligations under the convention, Parliament enacted several statutes for general and comprehensive regulation and control of aerial navigation in Canada. Four questions were referred to the Supreme Court of Canada regarding Parliament's exclusive legislative authority in respect of aeronautics.

The Supreme Court held that both Parliament and the provinces each had a field of jurisdiction in the subject area, and that the legislation in question exceeded the scope of Parliament's jurisdiction.

The Privy Council observed that the subject of transport was found both in ss. 91 and 92 of the British North America Act (the "BNA Act"), but that the subject of aeronautics was not specifically addressed. The Dominion attempted to justify the legislation under several classes of subjects found in s. 91, including regulation of trade and commerce, postal services, beacons, and navigation and shipping. On behalf of the provinces it was argued that aeronautics related to property and civil rights in the province or matters of a local or private nature. However, the Court held the matter to be governed by the power of Parliament and the Government of Canada to perform treaty obligations under s. 132 of the BNA Act.

Any small portion of the field not vested in the Dominion by specific words was also not vested in the provinces. Therefore, any such portion was held to belong to the Dominion under its power to legislate for peace, order and good government. In addition, the subject of aeronautics and the fulfilment of Canadian treaty obligations were held to be matters of national importance. The validity of the legislation was upheld and the appeal allowed.

86. *In re Regulation and Control of Radio Communication*
[1932] A.C. 304 (P.C.)

Canada ratified the International Radiotelegraph Convention, 1927 (the "Convention"), and enacted legislation in observation of its duties under the Convention. A reference was brought to the Supreme Court to determine if Parliament had the authority to regulate and control radio communication. A majority of the Court held that Parliament did have jurisdiction.

In referring to *Re Regulation and Control of Aeronautics (85)*, the Privy Council observed that the Convention in this case was not strictly a treaty as contemplated by s. 132 of the British NorthAmerica Act (the "BNA Act"). However, it amounted to the same thing. In any question of infringement of the Convention, the infringement would be committed not by the Dominion as a whole but by individuals within Canada. Regulation of such potential infringement by anyone in Canada could have been accomplished only by Dominion legislation.

On the subject of intraprovincial broadcasting, the Court looked to s. 92(10) of the BNA Act, which granted jurisdiction to the provinces for local works and undertakings. Broadcasting was interpreted as one of the exceptions contemplated by that provision, akin to "telegraphs" and being an "undertaking connecting the province with any other".

Even if it had been possible to make a sharp distinction between provincial and federal broadcasting, it was not possible to draw a sharp distinction between transmitters and receivers. Therefore, the Court rejected the argument that whereas a transmitter could be improperly used in such a way as to infringe the provisions of the Convention, a receiver could not be so used. The broadcasting system could not be divided into independent transmitting and receiving components, so jurisdiction rested entirely with the Dominion. The appeal was dismissed.

87. *Winner v. S.M.T. (Eastern) Ltd. and Attorney General of Canada*
[1951] S.C.R. 887, [1951] 4 D.L.R. 529

The appellant, W, was an American citizen who operated a bus line between Boston and Halifax. He was granted a licence under the Motor Carrier Act of New Brunswick to operate his buses within the province, but the licence forbade the taking on or letting off of passengers within the province. W operated his business in breach of that condition. The respondent, S, brought an action claiming an injunction restraining W from embussing and debussing passengers within the province, and claiming a declaration that W had no legal right to do so. S also sought damages.

The trial judge stayed the proceedings pending the answer by the Appellate Division of the Supreme Court of New Brunswick to questions of law raised by the proceedings. The questions concerned the validity of the Motor Carrier Act and whether W's operations were prohibited by that Act or by the Motor Vehicles Act. The Court held that the operations were prohibited by the legislation, which was valid.

W alleged that operation of his bus line between provinces and between Canada and the United States constituted an undertaking beyond the control of the provincial legislature. S contended that the province had the right to regulate without restriction all highway traffic regardless of origin or destination.

On appeal to the Supreme Court of Canada, the Court observed that it was concerned with an action rather than a reference, and thatthe questions involved the consideration of issues beyond those arising out of the action. The Court concluded that the Provincial Legislature had no power to forbid W from setting down or taking up passengers within the province. A majority of the members of the Court cited *In re Regulation and Control of Radio Communication (86)* for its definition that an undertaking "is not a physical thing but is an arrangement under which of course physical things are used". On that basis it was held that W's service was an interprovincial undertaking which came under federal jurisdiction.

88.   *Attorney General of Ontario v. Winner*
[1954] A.C. 541 (P.C.)

This was the appeal of *Winner v. S.M.T. (Eastern) Ltd. and Attorney General of Canada (87)*, in which the Privy Council extensively reviewed the concept of "undertaking" as contemplated by s. 92(10) of the British North America Act.

The Crown argued that something had to be both a work and an undertaking before it could be brought within the exceptions to provincial legislative authority. On the construction of the language used in s. 92, the Privy Council rejected this argument.

The Court cited *In re Regulation and Control of Radio Communication (86)* for its treatment of the word "undertaking", and dismissed the contention that an undertaking has no existence until potentially or actually carried into effect. The respondent W was found to be carrying on an undertaking extending beyond the limits of the province. Under s. 92(10) the Dominion was given legislative control of such undertakings. Although the province had authority over its own roads, such authority did not permit interference with undertakings extending beyond the limits of the province. Dominion jurisdiction extended to the undertaking rather than to the roads themselves, but legislation denying the use of provincial roads for such an undertaking was an interference with that jurisdiction.

The provincial legislation was not in pith and substance confined to traffic regulation. It was an interference with an undertaking connecting province and province. Therefore, it was an attempt to legislate in relation to a field reserved to Parliament.

In the Supreme Court of Canada it was held that although the provincial legislation could not prevent W from taking on passengers leaving the province or dropping off passengers entering the province, the legislation could prevent W from taking on or setting down passengers travelling solely between points within the province. The Privy Council, however, held that no such distinction could be made because W's undertaking was one and indivisible.

The Court concluded that it was not within the legislative powers of the province of New Brunswick to prohibit W from bringing passengers into the province and setting them down, or from picking up passengers and taking them out of the province, or from carrying passengers between points in New Brunswick.

89. *Reference re Industrial Relations and Disputes Investigation Act (Stevedoring Reference)*
[1955] S.C.R. 529

The Eastern Canada Stevedoring Co. was incorporated under the Companies Act of Canada and carried on operations in several provinces, one of which was Ontario. The company provided services in respect of loading and unloading ships and storing cargo. A union entered into two collective agreements with the company pursuant to a federal statute, the Industrial Relations and Disputes Investigation Act (the "IRDI Act"). Shortly before the execution of the second agreement another union filed an application with the Ontario Labour Relations Board (the "Board") for certification as the bargaining agent of the company's employees. The Board found that it had jurisdiction to hear the application on its merits under provincial labour legislation.

The first union sought to quash the decision of the Board or alternatively to prevent the Board from taking further proceedings. Once the constitutional validity of the federal Act became an issue, a reference was brought to the Supreme Court of Canada. The Court was asked if the IRDI Act applied to the Ontario employees of the Eastern Canada Stevedoring Co., and whether the IRDI Act was *ultra vires* Parliament.

A majority of the Court upheld the validity of the legislation and held that it did apply to the Ontario employees of the company. An earlier version of the IRDI Act had been struck down in *Toronto Electric Commissioners v. Snider (48)* as being in relation to property and civil rights in the province. However, it was subsequently re-enacted with a scope limited to those employees working "upon or in connection with the operation of any work, undertaking or business that is within the legislative authority of the Parliament of Canada".

The company declared that its operations consisted exclusively of services rendered in connection with the loading and unloading of ships that were operated on regular schedules between ports in Canada and ports outside Canada. That was a matter of federal legislative jurisdiction. The work done by stevedores was viewed as an integral part of the transportation of goods by water. Therefore, the legislation regulating their employment was justified under Parliament's jurisdiction over navigation and shipping as found in s. 91(10) of the British North America Act.

Rand J. held that the federal Act did not apply, saying that local labour relations could not be considered ancillary to Dominion power over shipping.

90. *Commission du Salaire Minimum v. Bell Telephone Co. of Canada*
[1966] S.C.R. 767, 59 D.L.R. (2d) 145

Under the Quebec Minimum Wage Act, the appellant, C, was permitted to impose a levy on employers based on a percentage of the wages paid to their employees. The respondent, B, contended that it was not subject to the levy because it was an undertaking coming within the jurisdiction of Parliament under s. 92(10) of the British North America Act. C brought an action to recover the amount of the levy it had imposed upon B. The action succeeded at trial but the decision was reversed on appeal.

It was conceded that B was an undertaking falling within the class defined in s. 92(10) and that the Minimum Wage Act had been validly enacted by the Provincial Legislature. The issue was whether or not the Act could apply to the kind of undertaking contemplated by s. 92(10).

The Supreme Court of Canada found that regulation and control of wages was a vital part of the B's commercial operation. Matters constituting a vital part of the operation of an interprovincial undertaking were held to be within exclusive federal jurisdiction. Since B was an interprovincial undertaking, the regulation of wages paid to its employees was a matter within the exclusive authority of Parliament. To the extent that the provincial Act purported to regulate wages paid by employers falling within exclusive federal jurisdiction, it was invalid. C's appeal was dismissed.

91. *Bell Canada v. Quebec (Commission de la Santé et de la Sécurité du Travail)*
[1988] 1 S.C.R. 749, 15 Q.A.C. 217

An employee of the appellant, B, applied for protective reassignment under provincial health and safety legislation. Her application was granted but the appellant presented a motion for evocation asking the Superior Court of Quebec to declare that the provincial Act did not apply to B as being a federal undertaking. The motion was granted, and the decision was affirmed by the Court of Appeal.

Beetz J. for a majority of the Supreme Court of Canada began by setting out five propositions to facilitate the analysis of the question. The first proposition stated that general legislative jurisdiction over health belonged to the provinces, subject to limited ancillary powers in Parliament to legislate for peace, order and good government. However, the Act was held to relate principally to working conditions, labour relations and the management of an undertaking, rather than to the subject matter of health. The first proposition was therefore inapplicable.

The second proposition stated that labour relations and working conditions fell within provincial jurisdiction as being matters of property and civil rights in the province. Therefore, the Act was valid. However, the third proposition provided for exclusive jurisdiction of Parliament over labour relations and working conditions where the jurisdiction was considered to be an integral part of the federal jurisdiction over another class of subjects. Therefore, under the decision of *Commission du Salaire Minimum v. Bell Telephone Co. of Canada (90)*, the Act could not apply to federal undertakings such as B.

The fourth proposition stated that provincial workers' compensation legislation applied to federal undertakings. The legislation in question in this case was primarily preventive rather than compensatory. Compensatory schemes were seen not to impinge on labour relations, working conditions, and management of undertakings. However, preventive schemes necessarily operated through labour relations, working conditions, and management of an undertaking. Therefore, compensatory schemes could be applied to federal undertakings, whereas preventive schemes could not.

The fifth proposition stated that as a consequence of the "double aspect" theory, Parliament and a province could enact two similar rules if the legislation had different purposes and distinct aspects. This had no application.

Therefore, the provincial legislation was held to be inapplicable to B, and the appeal was dismissed.

92.   *Irwin Toy Ltd. v. Quebec (Attorney General)*
   [1989] 1 S.C.R. 927, 39 C.R.R. 193

The Quebec Consumer Protection Act (the "Act") restricted advertising directed at persons under the age of 13. The appellant, I, broadcast messages which the Office de la protection du consommateur claimed were in breach of the Act. After several warnings from the office, I sought a declaration that the relevant sections of the Act were *ultra vires*. I alleged that the provisions were colourable legislation in that while they purported to restrict advertising aimed at children in all media, they specifically prohibited children's advertising on television. The trial judge upheld the Act as valid consumer protection legislation. On appeal, I alleged that the provisions infringed freedom of expression under the Charter of Rights. This argument was upheld by a majority and the provisions were declared to be inoperative.

An appeal was taken to the Supreme Court of Canada on the issues of whether the relevant provisions of the Act were within the legislative jurisdiction of the Quebec Legislature, whether the provisions were contrary to the Charter of Rights, and whether the provisions were protected from operation of the Charter by a legislative override provision.

The Supreme Court agreed with the trial judge that the Act was not a colourable attempt to legislate in relation to television advertising. Although there was evidence that television advertising was dominant, it was not the only form of children's advertising.

Advertising was found to be a vital part of the operation of a television broadcast undertaking. However, the provisions of the Act were aimed at advertisers and not at broadcasters. Therefore, the provisions did not purport to apply to a federal undertaking and did not trench on federal jurisdiction. The provisions might have incidentally affected the revenue of some television stations, but they did not impair the operation of a federal undertaking.

I argued that the provisions were in conflict with the federal regulations applicable to licensed broadcasters. However, the two regulatory schemes were interpreted as being compatible in that both broadcasters and advertisers could comply with their respective standards with no conflict arising. Thus the doctrine of paramountcy did not apply.

Because breach of the provisions had possible penal consequences, I contended that there was an encroachment on Parliament's criminal law power. However, the argument was rejected as the legislation was not in pith and substance in relation to criminal law.

Section 364 of the Consumer Protection Act provided that the Act was to operate notwithstanding ss. 2 and 7 to 15 of the Charter of Rights and Freedoms. The section ceased to have effect five years after it came into force and was not re-enacted. As a result, the legislative override was not in force at the time of the hearing of the appeal. The provisions of the Consumer Protection Act aimed at children's advertising were found to infringe the freedom of expression guaranteed by both the Canadian Charter and the Quebec Charter. However, the provisions were upheld as constituting a reasonable limit on freedom of expression.

93. *Alberta Government Telephones v. Canada (Canadian Radio-Television and Telecommunications Commission)*
[1989] 2 S.C.R. 225, 61 D.L.R. (4th) 193

The appellant, A, was created by provincial statute to operate a telephone system in the province. It later became a member of Telecom Canada, an unincorporated organization consisting of telecommunications companies operating in the other provinces. The operations of A grew to the point where its facilities were used to provide local, interprovincial and international services.

A second respondent, CNCP Telecommunications ("CNCP"), brought an application to the respondent C for various orders under the Railway Act requiring A to provide facilities for the interchange of communications traffic between CNCP's system and that of A. A subsequently applied to the Federal Court for a writ of prohibition. The Federal Court judge held that A was an interprovincial work or undertaking and thus fell within the legislative authority of Parliament. However, A was held to be an agent of the provincial Crown and thus could claim immunity from the provisions of the Railway Act, so the order of prohibition was granted. The Court of Appeal affirmed the finding that A was a federal undertaking but allowed the appeal on the issue of Crown immunity.

In the Supreme Court of Canada it was conceded that A was an "undertaking" within the meaning of s. 92(10) of the British North America Act, so the question was whether it was a "local" undertaking so as to be within provincial jurisdiction. Although the physical apparatus of the system was located in the province, the fact that the system taken as a whole connected the province with the rest of Canada and other parts of the world took it beyond the scope of a local undertaking. There was more than a mere physical connection with facilities of another province or state; A participated in various commercial arrangements organized in a manner which allowed it to provide interprovincial and international services to its local customers. The finding did not depend solely on A's relationship to Telecom Canada, for A itself was operating an interprovincial undertaking. However, A's role within the interprovincial framework of Telecom Canada was a relevant consideration.

On the issue of Crown immunity, A was found to be immune from jurisdiction under C exercised under the Railway Act. The appeal was allowed.

Criminal Law and Provincial Offences

94. *Quong-Wing v. The King*
(1914), 49 S.C.R. 440, 18 D.L.R. 121

A Saskatchewan statute prohibited the employment of white females in any business owned by "Oriental" persons. The appellant Q was a restaurant keeper who was convicted under this Act. His conviction was affirmed on appeal.

A majority of the Supreme Court of Canada dismissed the appeal. Duff J. began by dealing with the question of the jurisdiction of the Court to hear the appeal. The Criminal Code restricted appeals taken in a criminal case, but the words "criminal case" were interpreted narrowly so as not to include judgments in proceedings under provincial penal statutes.

Duff J. concluded that the legislation was in relation to matters of a local or private nature in the province, standing on the same footing as legislation prohibiting the sale of liquor. The fact that it prescribed penalties for a prohibited act did not necessarily make it criminal law. Classes 15 and 16 of s. 92 of the British North America Act allowed the provinces to suppress a provincial evil under the sanction of penalties. Furthermore, the legislation was not related to aliens and naturalization, since it was directed toward race and not nationality.

95. *Bédard v. Dawson*
[1923] S.C.R. 681, [1923] 4 D.L.R. 293

Quebec legislation made it an offence to use a building as a disorderly house. Anyone with reason to believe that a premises was being so used could apply for an injunction directed against an owner or occupier. The respondent, D, applied for an injunction against the appellant, B. B contended that the legislation was *ultra vires*, but the argument was rejected and the injunction granted. The Court of King's Bench by a majority upheld the constitutional validity of the legislation and dismissed the appeal.

The Supreme Court of Canada held that the legislation was concerned with the control and enjoyment of property rather than with the punishment of illegal acts. Therefore, it was in relation to property and civil rights in the province, and did not impinge on the federal criminal law power. The keeping of a disorderly house was an offence under the Criminal Code, but that did not prevent a province from legislating on the same matter with respect to civil rights.

96. *Reference re Validity of Section 5(a) of the Dairy Industry Act (Margarine Reference)*
[1949] S.C.R. 1, [1949] 1 D.L.R. 433

Section 5(*a*) of the federal Dairy Industry Act made it an offence to manufacture, import, sell, or possess any margarine, or any butter substitute manufactured wholly or in part from any fat other than that of milk or cream. A reference was brought to the Supreme Court of Canada to determine whether that section was *ultra vires* Parliament.

It was argued that the provision was within federal jurisdiction as being in relation to criminal law. **Proprietary Articles Trade Association v. Attorney General for Canada (57)** was cited for its broad definition of criminal law as involving acts prohibited by the state. However, it was necessary to examine that definition in the context of the legislation under consideration. An act would be prohibited by legislation for the purpose of addressing "some evil or injurious or undesirable effect upon the public" (Macklem, Risk, Rogerson, *et al.*, p. 376).

The object of the legislation in this case was seen not to relate to any purpose such as public peace, order, security, health or morality which would tend to support it as being in relation to criminal law. The objective was to give trade protection to the dairy industry. Insofar as the legislation restricted competitors of the dairy industry from manufacturing or selling the prohibited products in the provinces, it directly affected civil rights in the provinces. It was therefore *ultra vires* and did not become *intra vires* through the creation of offences and penalties.

However, that portion of the section which prohibited importation was valid. Importation was a matter of external trade, and therefore within the legislative authority of Parliament rather than the provinces.

An appeal to the Privy Council was dismissed ([1951] A.C. 179, [1950] 4 D.L.R. 689).

97. *Switzman v. Elbling and Attorney General of Quebec*
[1957] S.C.R. 285, 7 D.L.R. (2d) 337

Under Quebec legislation it was an offence for the occupier of a house to use it for the purpose of propagating communism or bolshevism by any means whatsoever. The Act Respecting Communist Propaganda provided for the closing of any house so used, and for imprisonment of anyone printing or publishing anything tending to propagate communism or bolshevism.

The respondent, E, leased premises to the appellant, S. S used the premises in a manner contrary to the Act and the house was closed. E brought an action to set aside the lease and to recover damages. In upholding E's action, the trial court held the Act to be *intra vires* the province. The decision was affirmed by the Court of Appeal. S appealed to the Supreme Court of Canada, raising a dispute between S and the Attorney General of the province on the issue of the validity of the statute.

A majority of the Court allowed the appeal. The Act was held to be in relation to criminal law such that the province had no legislative authority. The case of *Bédard v. Dawson (95)* was distinguished. That case dealt with the control and enjoyment of property, where the legislature provided for civil consequences of a criminal act. The purpose of the legislation in this case was to protect the public against the propagation of communist propaganda, with the legislature purporting to create a crime.

In dissent, Taschereau J. held that the legislature had not made communism a crime punishable by law. Rather, it had made laws in relation to the possession and use of property, to achieve the aim of crime prevention. That was a valid exercise of its power to make laws in relation to property and civil rights.

98. *R. v. Chief*
(1963), 42 D.L.R. (2d) 712 (Man. Q.B.)

The defendants, C, were charged under s. 127 of the provincial Child Welfare Act with neglecting their children in a manner likely to cause suffering or injury. They applied to quash the information on the grounds that the relevant section of the Act encroached on the field of criminal law and that the field of child neglect had been occupied by the Criminal Code. The Child Welfare Act provided for a term of imprisonment for up to five years for neglect of a child under 18 years of age. The relevant section of the Criminal Code imposed a duty on a parent or guardian to provide necessaries of life for a child under age 16, and made it an offence for anyone subject to that duty to fail to perform it.

The Court held that in pith and substance the purpose of s. 127 was to aid the better enforcement of the Act and to secure the proper treatment of children by safeguarding their care, custody and behaviour. The section did not have the purpose of creating offences, and thus did not encroach upon the field of criminal law.

The Criminal Code had not occupied the field as it created a specific offence relating to conduct which was much narrower in scope than that set out in s. 127. The Court viewed the facts of the case as possibly involving neglect, but probably not involving a failure to provide necessaries of life. Even if the circumstances of a particular case came within the scope of both federal and provincial provisions, there would not necessarily be a conflict leading to the suspension of the provincial enactment. The application was dismissed.

An appeal to the Manitoba Court of Appeal was dismissed (((1964), 44 D.L.R. (2d) 108).

99. *Morgentaler v. The Queen*
[1976] 1 S.C.R. 616, 53 D.L.R. (3d) 161

The appellant, M, was acquitted by a jury of the charge of unlawfully procuring a miscarriage, contrary to s. 251 of the Criminal Code. The verdict was set aside and a conviction entered by the Quebec Court of Appeal. The Court of Appeal held that the common law defence of necessity and the defence under s. 45 of the Criminal Code were not available as defences to charges under s. 251. Section 45 protected from criminal responsibility anyone who performed an operation with reasonable care and skill if, under the circumstances, it was reasonable to perform the operation.

An appeal was brought to the Supreme Court of Canada on several grounds. The majority affirmed the decision of the Court of Appeal that the s. 45 defence and the common law defence were not available. Further, the Criminal Code authorized the Court of Appeal to enter a guilty verdict after acquittal by a jury. The power was to be exercised with caution, but it was applicable in this case where the accused admitted commission of the offence and relied on defences which were found to be unavailable. The appeal was dismissed.

There was an argument that s. 251 encroached upon provincial legislative jurisdiction in relation to hospitals and the medical profession. The argument was addressed by the dissenting judges, speaking through Laskin C.J. The relationship of s. 251 to the establishment of hospitals or the regulation of the medical profession was seen to be incidental. The provisions of s. 251 were within the scope of what constitutes a valid exercise of the criminal law power as discussed in *Reference re Validity of Section 5(a) of the Dairy Industry Act (Margarine Reference) (96)*. The fact that Parliament had equated the interference of the ordinary course of conception with socially undesirable and punishable conduct was a valid exercise of its criminal law power. However, the dissenting judges upheld the availability of the defences and would have allowed the appeal.

100. *R. v. Morgentaler (1993)*
[1993] 3 S.C.R. 463, 107 D.L.R. (4th) 537

In Nova Scotia, provincial regulations prohibited abortions anywhere other than in a hospital, and denied insurance coverage for abortions performed outside a hospital. The respondent, M, opened a free-standing abortion clinic in the province and performed abortions there. He was charged with unlawfully performing a designated medical service other than in a hospital contrary to the Medical Services Act.

The trial judge held that the provincial legislation was in pith and substance criminal law and thus *ultra vires*. There was a provincial objective of eliminating privatization of health care services, but this was incidental to the primary purpose of keeping abortion clinics out of the province. M was acquitted. A majority of the Court of Appeal agreed with the conclusions of the trial judge and dismissed the appeal.

An appeal was brought to the Supreme Court of Canada on the issue of whether the provincial Act and regulations were *ultra vires* as legislation in relation to criminal law.

The Supreme Court acknowledged that the province had the legislative authority to pass a law preventing privatization of designated services. However, the legislation in this case prohibited abortions in certain circumstances and attached penal consequences. It was therefore suspect on its face as legislation prohibiting conduct historically viewed as criminal.

The legal effect of the provincial legislation was seen to overlap that of s. 251 of the Criminal Code, which had been struck down in *R. v. Morgentaler (1988) (141)* as violating the right to life, liberty and security of the person. The overlap of legal effects supported the inference that the provincial legislation was designed to serve a criminal law purpose.

The Court reviewed evidence that the legislation was the government's response to M's stated intention to set up a free-standing abortion clinic in the province. Legislative debates excerpted from Hansard indicated an interest in maintaining public morals, creating a strong inference that the legislation was in relation to criminal law. The evidence further suggested that privatization and quality and cost of health services were merely incidental concerns. Therefore, the legislation could not be supported under any of the heads of provincial jurisdiction found in s. 92 of the British North America Act.

Reference re Validity of Section 5(a) of the Dairy Industry Act (Margarine Reference) (96) was cited to hold that the presence or absence of a criminal public purpose or object was pivotal to the characterization of legislation as criminal. The Court concluded that the primary objective of the legislation was the prohibition of socially undesirable conduct in the form of abortions performed outside hospitals. It was an invasion of the field of criminal law and thus *ultra vires* in its entirety.

101. *Nova Scotia Board of Censors v. McNeil*
[1978] 2 S.C.R. 662, 55 D.L.R. (3d) 632

The appellant, N, was established under the provincial Theatres and Amusements Act. All films exhibited in the province had to be submitted to and authorized by N. The Act granted authority to N to prohibit the use or exhibition of any film. N banned the film *Last Tango in Paris* from public viewing anywhere in the province.

The respondent, M, brought an application for a declaration that certain sections of the Act and regulations made thereunder were *ultra vires*. The questions raised in the application were referred to the Appeal Division of the Nova Scotia Supreme Court, who held the provisions to be *ultra vires* on the ground that they invaded federal criminal law power.

The majority of the Supreme Court of Canada found the legislation to be primarily directed to the regulation, supervision and control of the film business in the province. As such it was within provincial jurisdiction as being in relation to property and civil rights in the province. The legislation was not concerned with creating a criminal offence or providing for punishment. The rejection of films was based on a failure to conform to N's standards of propriety. The provincial government was regulating a local trade and in doing so was allowed to set its own standards which in no way excluded the operation of the Criminal Code.

The order of the Appeal Division expressly stated that the use of the word "prohibiting" in the legislation was the basis of the holding that the provisions were *ultra vires*. However, the majority of the Supreme Court held that since the legislation itself had been enacted for a valid provincial purpose, the prohibition was also valid.

Regulation 32 of the provincial legislation prohibited indecent or improper performances. This provision was seen to be indistinguishable from s. 159 of the Criminal Code, and was thus invalid as invading federal criminal law power. However, the provision was severable, and thus the remainder of the legislation was upheld.

The dissenting judges held that this was a case of a provincially authorized tribunal defining and determining what was permissible and what was not, which was a direct intrusion into the field of criminal law.

102. *Attorney General for Canada and Dupond v. Montreal*
[1978] 2 S.C.R. 770, 84 D.L.R. (3d) 420

Under a City of Montreal By-law the Executive Committee of the city was authorized to prohibit the holding of assemblies, parades or gatherings if such activities engendered reasonable grounds to anticipate danger to safety, peace or public order. Pursuant to the by-law the Executive Committee passed an ordinance prohibiting the holding of any assembly, parade or gathering on the public domain of the city for a period of 30 days.

The validity of the legislation was attacked by the appellant, D, as a ratepayer of the city. The trial judge found some overlap between the provisions of the by-law and the Criminal Code, and concluded that the by-law was *ultra vires* as being in relation to criminal law. The Court of Appeal viewed the by-law and ordinance as local police regulations and allowed the appeal.

A majority of the Supreme Court of Canada characterized the by-law and ordinance as regulations of a merely local character. The ordinance was a temporary measure and was passed for reasons peculiar to the city at the relevant time. The enactments related to a matter of a merely local or private nature in the province. They were preventive rather than punitive measures, and as such did not relate to criminal law. The legislation was valid and the appeal was dismissed.

Laskin C.J. speaking for the dissenting judges held that the provisions were so explicitly directed to breach of the peace and to the maintenance of public order that they fell squarely within criminal law power. The prohibition of all gatherings, including those for innocent purposes, was described as something "which should alarm free citizens" even if invoked under the wide criminal law authority of the Parliament of Canada.

Property and Civil Rights

103. *Cunningham v. Tomey Homma*
[1903] A.C. 151 (P.C.)

The respondent, T, a naturalized Japanese, sought to be placed on the register of voters for the electoral district of Vancouver City. Provincial electoral law forbade Japanese, whether naturalized or not, from voting and from having their names appear on the register. The appellant C refused to enter T's name on the register in accordance with the provincial law. An application to overrule C's decision was granted by the Chief Justice of the County Court. The Supreme Court of British Columbia dismissed the appeal.

On appeal to the Privy Council, it was observed that the provincial law had nothing to do with aliens and naturalization, for a child born in Canada to Japanese parents would have been excluded from voting under the provisions of the Act. Under s. 91(25) of the British North America Act it was for Parliament to determine the constituents, but not the consequences, of alienage or naturalization. The provincial legislature was entitled to exclude residents of the province from the right to vote in the province. Privileges that depended on residence were independent of nationality. The legislation was held to be validly enacted under s. 92(1), allowing the province to amend its own constitution. The appeal was allowed.

104. *Morgan v. Attorney General for Prince Edward Island*
[1976] 2 S.C.R. 349, 55 D.L.R. (3d) 527

The Real Property Act of Prince Edward Island permitted citizens of countries other than Canada to acquire, hold and sell real property in the province. Anyone not resident in the province required permission of the Lieutenant-Governor-in-Council to acquire more than 10 acres. For the purposes of the relevant section, residence was defined by the Act itself and citizenship was defined by the Canadian Citizenship Act.

The appellant, M, was a citizen and resident of the United States. M challenged the validity of the legislation. The challenge was rejected by the Supreme Court of Prince Edward Island.

The Supreme Court of Canada interpreted the relevant section as applying to Canadian citizens residing outside of the province, as well as to aliens residing outside of the province. The power of the province to regulate land use by limiting the amount of land that could be held was not contested. However, it was contended that the legislation created a situation where nonresidents would be disadvantaged as against residents. Consequently, the legislation was in pith and substance in relation to citizenship and thus *ultra vires*. This argument was rejected. No one was prevented from entering the province and taking up residence. The residency requirement of the section affected both aliens and citizens alike and related to the valid provincial object of limiting the size of holdings of land in the province. The appeal was dismissed.

105. *Interprovincial Co-operatives Ltd. v. The Queen in Right of Manitoba*
(1975), [1976] 1 S.C.R. 477, 53 D.L.R. (3d) 321

Manitoba legislation created liability against any person discharging a contaminant "into waters in the province or into any water whereby it is carried into waters in the province". The statute provided that it would not be a defence to show that the discharge was permitted by the regulatory authority having jurisdiction where the discharge occurred.

An action was brought against the appellant I for damage to the province's fisheries resulting from discharge of pollutants from plants in Saskatchewan and Ontario into waters flowing into Manitoba. I moved to strike, contending that the Act was *ultra vires* the province. The motion was granted at trial but the decision was reversed by the Court of Appeal.

A majority of the Supreme Court of Canada allowed the appeal. Three judges of seven, speaking through Pigeon J., observed that although the legislation was aimed at damage caused in Manitoba, it was not directed at acts done in the province. The province owned the inland fisheries in its territory and was entitled to legislate for the protection of its property. However, it did not have legislative authority over acts done in another province. Therefore, Manitoba was restricted to remedies available at common law or under federal legislation.

Ritchie J. concurred in the result but expressly rejected the reasoning. I's civil rights stemmed from licences granted in Ontario and Saskatchewan. The Crown's claim for an injunction restraining I from discharging pollutants into rivers in Ontario or Saskatchewan was an attempt to assert a right to enter another province and invoke Manitoba law.

Laskin C.J. spoke for the three dissenting judges who held that the cause of action arose in Manitoba, even though the cause of damage may have arisen outside Manitoba. The appellant sought an immunity in Manitoba based on a licence to pollute granted outside the province. Such a licence could not provide a defence against liability for injury to Manitoba property.

Civil and Criminal Procedure

106. *Valin v. Langlois*
(1879), 3 S.C.R. 1

Under the Dominion Controverted Elections Act, the respondent, L, brought a petition against the election of the appellant, V, to a seat in the House of Commons. V objected to the petition, but the objections were dismissed by the Superior Court for Lower Canada. It was held that the Act was not *ultra vires* Parliament. The Act could validly impose on a Superior Court the duty of trying controverted elections of members of the House of Commons.

On appeal, the Supreme Court of Canada held that it was within the competence of Parliament to confer on provincial courts the power and authority to deal with controverted elections. Conferring such power did not affect provincial autonomy regarding property and civil rights and administration of justice in the province. The provincial courts were required to execute all laws, whether passed by Parliament or by provincial legislatures. Parliament was allowed to impose a new jurisdiction or mode of procedure on the provincial courts in relation to any subject area within its legislative power. The appeal from the decision of the Superior Court was dismissed.

107. *Batary v. Attorney General for Saskatchewan*
[1965] S.C.R. 465, 52 D.L.R. (2d) 125

After the commencement of a coroner's inquest the appellant, B, and eight others were separately charged with the murder of the deceased. Under s. 8a of the provincial Coroners Act the Coroner closed the inquest, but the Attorney General reopened it pursuant to the same section. The Crown intended to call B and the other accused as witnesses at the inquest. The accused contended that neither the Crown nor the Coroner could compel any of them to be sworn as a witnesses.

The Coroner ruled that each of the accused was a compellable witness at the inquest. B brought an application for prohibition, which was dismissed. B appealed, saying that the Coroner's Court was a Criminal Court of Record and that the relevant sections of the Coroners Act were *ultra vires* as being in relation to criminal law. The Court of Appeal held that the provisions were in relation to the administration of justice in the province rather than in relation to criminal law, and dismissed the appeal.

A majority of the Supreme Court of Canada allowed B's appeal. Historically, a person charged with murder and awaiting trial could not be compelled to testify at the inquest into the deceased's death. Neither the Evidence Act nor the Criminal Code had brought about a change in the state of the law. An earlier version of the

Coroners Act provided that a person charged with an offence relating to the deceased's death could not be compellable to give evidence at an inquest. However, that provision had been removed when the Act was amended. The Court viewed the change as an attempt to alter the rules designed to protect the accused. This was held to be legislation in relation to criminal law including procedure in criminal matters. The provisions were therefore *ultra vires*.

108. *R. v. Hauser*
[1979] 1 S.C.R. 984, 98 D.L.R. (3d) 193

The respondent, H, had been charged with possession of a narcotic for the purpose of trafficking. The indictment was signed by an agent of the Attorney General of Canada. H moved for an order of prohibition, alleging that criminal procedure was a provincial matter. The application for prohibition was dismissed, but granted on appeal. The Crown appealed to the Supreme Court of Canada on the issues of whether Parliament could enact legislation to authorize the Attorney General of Canada to prefer indictments for offences under the Narcotics Control Act, and to have conduct of proceedings in respect of a violation of any Act of Parliament other than the Criminal Code.

A majority of the Court held that s. 91(29) of the British North America Act created a federal power, independent of criminal law power, to provide for the imposition of penalties for the violation of any federal legislation. Therefore, notwithstanding provincial jurisdiction over administration of justice in criminal matters, there was unrestricted federal legislative authority over prosecutions for violations of those federal enactments deriving their constitutional validity from other than the criminal law power.

The Court reviewed the history of narcotic control legislation to conclude that it was legislation adopted to deal with a problem not contemplated at the time of Confederation. Therefore, it was not enacted under the criminal law power. Just as in *Re Regulation and Control of Aeronautics (85)* and *In re Regulation and Control of Radio Communication (86)*, it was enacted under the general residual federal power. As such, Parliament did have authority to conduct the proceedings and the Attorney General was allowed to prefer indictments for offences under the Narcotics Control Act. The appeal was allowed.

The dissenting judges held that the Attorney General of the province had exclusive authority in respect of federal statutes which were in pith and substance criminal law. The Narcotic Control Act was such a law, therefore it was not within the competence of Parliament to enact legislation authorizing the Attorney General of Canada to institute proceedings, prefer indictments, and conduct prosecutions under the Act.

See also *Attorney General for Canada v. Canadian National Transportaion Ltd. (68)*

Marriage and Divorce

109. *In re Marriage Legislation in Canada*
[1912] A.C. 880 (P.C.)

A federal bill proposed to amend the Marriage Act such that every ceremony of marriage performed according to local laws would be deemed to be a valid marriage everywhere in Canada. Further, no canonical decree or custom of any province could invalidate or qualify any such marriage or any of the rights of the married persons or their children. A question was submitted to the Supreme Court of Canada to determine to what extent these provisions were within the legislative authority of Parliament. A second question asked whether the law of the province of Quebec rendered null and void any marriage in which at least one of the parties was Roman Catholic, but the ceremony was not performed by a Roman Catholic priest. If the second question was answered in the affirmative, a third question asked whether Parliament had the authority to enact that such a marriage be legal and binding.

The Supreme Court of Canada held the federal bill to be *ultra vires*. The marriages described in the second question were held to be valid. The legislation described in the third question was seen to be beyond the authority of Parliament.

The Privy Council considered whether the provincial power over solemnization of marriage in the province was restricted to the regulation of formalities and did not extend to any question of validity. The provincial power was viewed as an exception to the federal power over marriage and divorce, such that the jurisdiction of Parliament did not cover the whole field of validity. The province had exclusive capacity to determine who could perform valid marriage ceremonies. Prior to Confederation the concept of solemnization as ordinarily understood included conditions affecting the validity of the marriage contract. Therefore, it was held that the concept as understood was imported into the British North America Act. Since the purpose of the bill was to allow any person with authority to validly perform a marriage ceremony irrespective of the religious faith of the persons being married, the bill was held to be *ultra vires* and it was unnecessary to answer the other two questions.

110. *Zacks v. Zacks*
[1973] S.C.R. 891, 35 D.L.R. (3d) 420

The respondent petitioned for divorce from his wife, the appellant. The wife sought interim and permanent maintenance for herself and her daughter. A decree *nisi* for divorce was granted, and it was ordered that the respondent and the daughter were entitled to maintenance. The Registrar conducted a hearing for the purpose of recommending an amount. Before the hearing had been completed the respondent obtained a decree absolute. He then applied for an order to stay the proceedings before the Registrar but the application was dismissed.

The Registrar made several interim recommendations for payment. The appellant applied before a judge to require the respondent to pay the sums, and the respondent applied for a declaration that the Registrar was without jurisdiction. The appellant's application was granted and the respondent's dismissed. The respondent appealed and the decision was reversed. The Court of Appeal said that once the decree *nisi* had been perfected nothing, such as fixing lump sums or periodic sums, could be done later.

A further appeal was brought to the Supreme Court of Canada on the issue of whether ss. 10, 11 and 12 of the Divorce Act were *ultra vires* Parliament. Those sections gave a court granting relief on a divorce petition power to make interim orders for the payment of alimony and maintenance, and to make orders for the payment of lump sums to the spouse and children. Any such orders could be varied or rescinded by the court, or could be made subject to conditions. A second question directed to the Court asked whether an Order-in-Council, allowing a judge on an application for corollary relief to direct a reference to the Registrar, was *ultra vires* as constituting an unlawful delegation to a person other than a judge appointed under s. 96 of the British North America Act (the "BNA Act").

In answering the first question the Supreme Court observed that alimony, maintenance and custody of children were not specifically mentioned in either s. 91 or s. 92 of the BNA Act. The subjects were in relation to civil rights and could have been supported under provincial power to legislate in respect of property and civil rights in the province. However, they were held to be inseparable from the direct consequence of marriage and its dissolution, over which Parliament had exclusive legislative jurisdiction.

In answer to the second question, the Court held that the power conferred on the Registrar was one of inquiry and recommendation, rather than one of adjudication. The Order-in-Council was thus not *ultra vires*.

In deciding on the merits, the Court found that the issue of amount of maintenance was a complicated matter which could not be ascertained immediately. The hearing before the Registrar was an extension of the order declaring entitlement to maintenance. Thus, the judge did not have to fix the actual amount of maintenance at the time of the granting of the decree *nisi*. The appeal was allowed and the decision of the trial judge restored.

Natural Resources

111. *Attorney General for the Dominion of Canada v. Attorneys General for Ontario, Quebec and Nova Scotia (Fisheries)*
[1898] A.C. 700 (P.C.)

Several questions were referred to the Supreme Court of Canada relating to the property, rights, and legislative jurisdiction of Canada and the provinces with respect to rivers, lakes, harbours and fisheries. As there was divided success between the Dominion and the provinces, both parties appealed the decision of the Supreme Court.

The Privy Council began with two preliminary observations. First, the rights of the public in respect of Crown property would be the same regardless of whether the property was found to vest in the province or in the Dominion. Second, legislative jurisdiction over a particular subject matter did not necessarily correspond to proprietary rights.

One question asked whether the beds of all lakes, rivers, public harbours, and other waters situate within the territorial limits of the provinces became Dominion property under the British North America Act (the "BNA Act"). The Third Schedule of the BNA Act listed "rivers and lakes improvements" as one of the "Provincial Public Works and Property to be the Property of Canada". The Privy Council rejected the contention that the word "improvements" was attached only to the word "lakes", and that the rivers themselves were the property of Canada. It was held that the improvements alone, for both the rivers and lakes, were transferred to the Dominion.

On the issue of public harbours, the Third Schedule explicitly vested those in the Dominion. The Court declined to attempt an exhaustive definition of "public harbour", considering that to be a matter which would depend on the circumstances of each case.

With respect to fisheries and fishing rights, the Dominion was granted legislative jurisdiction but not proprietary rights. Specific Dominion legislation purporting to grant fishery leases conferring a right to fish in property belonging to the provinces was held to be *ultra vires*, as the Dominion could not confer property rights where it had none itself. Generally, however, enactment of fishery regulations was within the competence of Parliament alone.

112. *Reference re Ownership of Offshore Mineral Rights*
[1967] S.C.R. 792, 65 D.L.R. (2d) 353

Two questions were referred to the Supreme Court of Canada to determine whether Canada or British Columbia had proprietary and exploratory rights to and legislative jurisdiction over the lands and natural resources of the territorial sea off the coast of British Columbia, and whether Canada or British Columbia had such rights over the continental shelf.

British Columbia took the position that at the time the province was created it included the territorial sea. Canada argued that land below the low-water mark was not part of the colony before Confederation and did not become part of the province after Confederation.

The Supreme Court reviewed the history of the area to conclude that before Confederation all unalienated lands in British Columbia belonged to the Crown in the right of the Colony of British Columbia. After Confederation the lands remained vested in the Crown in right of the province. Originally, any rights in the territorial sea were asserted by the British Crown in respect of the Dominion of Canada. Pursuant to the Statute of Westminster, Canada asserted its own rights in the territorial sea. The Territorial Sea and Fishing Zones Act of 1964, together with the Geneva Convention of 1958, defined Canada's sovereignty over the territorial sea.

On the basis of the Court's historical analysis it was concluded that at no time had the colony or the province of British Columbia any property in the bed of the territorial sea. The sovereign state of Canada had the right to explore and exploit the lands and had exclusive legislative jurisdiction under s. 91 of the British North America Act.

With respect to the continental shelf, it was held that international law did not extend the limits of the territorial sea. The continental shelf was outside the boundaries of British Columbia, and Canada was the sovereign state recognized under the Geneva Convention as having rights and obligations with respect to the continental shelf.

As such, both questions were answered in favour of Canada.

113. *Central Canada Potash Co. Ltd. v. Government of Saskatchewan*
[1979] 1 S.C.R. 42, 88 D.L.R. (3d) 609

The Saskatchewan potash industry was heavily dependent on an export market. Facing financial difficulty, the industry sought protection from the provincial government. Consequently, a potash prorationing scheme was developed for the purpose of regulating the marketing of potash through fixed minimum prices and production quotas. Under the scheme the appellant, C, encountered difficulty in fulfilling its contractual commitments. C brought an action for damages in tort and for a declaration that the prorationing scheme was invalid. The scheme was held to be invalid at trial, but the decision was reversed by the Court of Appeal.

The Supreme Court of Canada observed that although control of natural resources in a province was ordinarily within the legislative jurisdiction of the province, provincial jurisdiction did not extend to the control or marketing of natural resources in interprovincial or export trade. The "true nature and character" of the legislation in this case was regulation of the export price of potash.

The Court of Appeal held that, if the right to control production of potash within the province and to establish a minimum price did not rest with the province, it had to rest with Parliament; however, such powers clearly did not rest with Parliament. The Supreme Court rejected this line of reasoning. The issue was limitation on provincial power, and a holding that provincial legislation was invalid did not move the power to Parliament. The legislation was declared to be *ultra vires*, but the appellant's claim for damages for the tort of intimidation was dismissed.

Aboriginal Claims

114. *St. Catherine's Milling and Lumber Company v. The Queen*
   (1888), 14 App. Cas. 46 (P.C.)

The Government of Canada entered into a treaty with the Salteaux band whereby a large tract of land was surrendered to the "Government of the Dominion, for Her Majesty and her successors". The Salteaux retained hunting and fishing rights throughout the territory, with the exception of those portions required for purposes such as settlement, mining and lumbering. Subsequently, the Crown Timber Agent of the Dominion Government issued a lumbering permit to the appellant S. The permit affected a portion of the treaty land located in the Province of Ontario.

The Ontario government contended that under the treaty the land in question had vested in the Crown in right of the province. The province brought an action for an injunction restraining the appellant from cutting any timber on the lands specified in the licence and from removing any timber already cut, for a declaration that the appellant had no rights in respect of the timber, and for damages. The action succeeded at trial and was affirmed by both the Ontario Court of Appeal and the Supreme Court of Canada.

The Privy Council observed that s. 102 of the British North America Act provided that duties and revenues raised under provincial jurisdiction were to be paid into a Consolidated Revenue Fund for the Public Service of Canada. However, there was an exception under s. 109 which provided that all lands, mines, minerals, and royalties belonging to the several provinces, and all sums due and payable for such lands, mines, minerals, and royalties, would belong to the several provinces, subject to any interest other than that of the province. Before the treaty, the Crown had a proprietary interest in the land subject to the aboriginal interest. The aboriginal interest was surrendered with the treaty. On that basis, it was held that each province had been given the entire beneficial interest of the Crown in all lands within its boundaries.

The Court rejected the argument that federal legislative power over aboriginals and their lands implied a federal proprietary interest in reserved lands. The Court also rejected the argument that the treaty involved a conveyance to the Dominion Government. The terms of the treaty clearly indicated a transaction between the Salteaux and the Crown. The revenues derived from the lands in question were held to be the property of the Province of Ontario and the Dominion had no power to dispose of Ontario's beneficial interest in the timber, even though the Dominion retained exclusive power to regulate hunting and fishing privileges. The appeal was dismissed.

115. *Calder v. Attorney General of British Columbia*
[1973] S.C.R. 313, 34 D.L.R. (3d) 145

The appellant C sued as a representative of the Nishga Indian Band for a declaration that "the aboriginal title . . . of the plaintiffs to their ancient tribal territory . . . ha[d] never been lawfully extinguished" (at 313 S.C.R.). The territory in question was located in northwestern British Columbia. The action was dismissed at trial and on appeal.

On further appeal, the Supreme Court was divided. Three judges speaking through Judson J. held that the geographical limits of the Royal Proclamation of 1763 did not extend to the land in question. Therefore, the appellant could not claim the benefits of the provisions of the Proclamation. According to the historical evidence, including a series of proclamations and ordinances of the colonial government, "the sovereign authority elected to exercise complete dominion over the lands in question, adverse to any right of occupancy which the Nishga Tribe might have had, when, by legislation, it opened up such lands for settlement, subject to the reserves of land set aside for Indian occupation." (at 344 S.C.R.) The action failed and the appeal was dismissed.

Pigeon J. dismissed the appeal on a point of jurisdiction. The granting of a fiat of the Lieutenant-Governor of the province under the Crown Procedure Act was a prerequisite to bringing an action for a declaration claiming title against the Crown in right of the province. The fiat had not been granted, therefore the Court had no jurisdiction to make the declaratory order.

The remaining three judges, speaking through Hall J., would have allowed the appeal. It was held that the Royal Proclamation of 1763 did apply to establish aboriginal title to the lands in question. The title, once established, could not be extinguished except by surrender to the Crown or by specific legislation. The Nishgas had not surrendered their title. There was no legislation from the colony, nor from the province, nor from Parliament, extinguishing the title. On the jurisdictional issue, a petition for declaratory relief was held not to be the kind of action within the rule requiring a fiat.

116. *Guerin v. The Queen*
[1984] 2 S.C.R. 335, 13 D.L.R. (4th) 321

The appellant, G, was the Chief of the Musqueam Band. The members of the band lived on a reserve located within the City of Vancouver. The Indian Affairs Branch was aware that the land was very valuable. A representative of a golf club approached the Indian Affairs Branch and submitted a proposal to lease a portion of the reserve. Ultimately, the band members held a meeting to vote to surrender the land to the Crown for the purpose of lease to the golf club. The band subsequently brought an action for damages, claiming that several terms and conditions of the lease were different from those disclosed to them before the surrender vote and that some of the lease terms were not disclosed at all. The trial judge found that the Crown was in breach of trust and awarded damages. The Crown's appeal was allowed.

The Supreme Court of Canada allowed the appeal. Dickson J. speaking for three judges held that the Crown's position with respect to the band could not be defined as a trust. Aboriginal title existed independently of the Royal Proclamation of 1763. The title was the same for interest in a reserve as for interest in traditional tribal lands. The nature of the title did not amount to a beneficial ownership, but in cases of surrender it did give rise to a fiduciary obligation on the part of the Crown to deal with the land for the benefit of the surrendering Indians. Although s. 18(1) of the Indian Act conferred on the Crown a broad discretion in dealing with surrendered land, the discretion was subject to the Crown's fiduciary obligation. In this case, the Crown's agents promised the band to lease the land on specified terms. After the land had been surrendered, the terms of the lease were altered so that it was much less valuable. The Crown therefore breached its fiduciary duty and was liable in damages.

Wilson J. for three judges held that while s. 18 of the Indian Act did not create a fiduciary obligation, it did recognize the existence of the obligation. The fiduciary duty on the Crown crystallized upon surrender into an express trust of specific land for a specific purpose. When the Crown proceeded with a lease on terms which were not acceptable to the band, it was in breach of trust.

Estey J. disposed of the appeal on the basis of the law of agency. The Crown, under the direction and for the benefit of the band, were agents for the band for the purpose of developing and exploiting their interest in the land. The Crown representatives failed to carry out their instructions and were liable for the breach.

Treaties

117. *Attorney General for Canada v. Attorney General for Ontario*
     (Labour Conventions Case)
     [1937] A.C. 326 (P.C.)

Parliament passed three statutes concerning labour law, in compliance with the conventions which had been adopted by the International Labour Organization of the League of Nations in accordance with the Labour Part of the Treaty of Versailles of 1919. The Dominion admitted that each statute affected property and civil rights in each of the provinces, but contended that the legislation was valid under s. 132 of the British North America Act as being necessary for performing treaty obligations as part of the British Empire. Alternatively, it was alleged that the legislation was valid under the federal residuary power to make laws for peace, order and good government. The provinces contended that any obligations of Canada did not arise under any treaty made between the Empire and foreign countries, that the Canadian Government had no authority to make any such treaty as alleged, that the obligations incurred and the powers exercised were not done so in accordance with the Treaty of Versailles, and that the residuary power could not save the legislation as it related to property and civil rights in the province. The question of the validity of the legislation was brought to the Supreme Court of Canada, where six members of the Court were divided equally.

On appeal, the Privy Council observed a distinction between the formation and the performance of obligations constituted by a treaty between two or more sovereign states. Formation of a treaty was an executive act, while performance of obligations depended on legislative action. The Court acceded to the argument that the obligations did not arise under a treaty between the British Empire and foreign countries. The obligations were those of Canada "by virtue of her new status as an international person" (at 349 A.C.), so that s. 132 did not apply. The Court therefore declined to comment on the arguments concerning the Canadian Government's executive authority.

In addressing the Dominion's alternative argument, the Court held that for the purposes of distribution of legislative powers, there was no such thing as treaty legislation. It was necessary to assess a particular treaty to determine which class of subject it dealt with, in order to ascertain appropriate legislative authority. By acquiring international status the Dominion acquired an increased scope of executive functions but acquired no greater legislative competence. In this case each of the three Acts dealt with property and civil rights in the province, and thus each of them were *ultra vires* Parliament.

118. *Schneider v. The Queen*
[1982] 2 S.C.R. 112, 139 D.L.R. (3d) 417

The Heroin Treatment Act of British Columbia set up a comprehensive pro-
gramme for the evaluation, treatment and rehabilitation of those dependent on
narcotics. The Act provided that where a peace officer had reasonable grounds to
believe that a person had a dependency on a narcotic, the peace officer could require the person to submit to an examination. Noncompliance with such a notice
could result in the person being taken into custody for detention in a treatment
centre. The appellant, S, brought an action to declare the Act unconstitutional.
The trial judge held the Act to be *ultra vires* but the decision was reversed by the
Court of Appeal.

S contended that the Act was in pith and substance legislation in relation to narcotics and thus within the exclusive jurisdiction of Parliament, either under the
treaty making power or under the power to make laws for the peace, order and
good government of Canada. Alternatively, the Act was in pith and substance legislation in relation to criminal law and was within the exclusive jurisdiction of
Parliament. In the further alternative, if the legislation was valid it was rendered
inoperative by federal legislation.

The Supreme Court of Canada dismissed the appeal. The subject of narcotics was
held to be not "so global and indivisible that the legislative domain cannot be divided" (Whyte, Lederman & Bur, p. 17-13). Illegal trade in narcotics was within
the jurisdiction of Parliament. However, the Heroin Treatment Act was not in relation to the control of narcotic drugs. There was nothing to indicate that the problem of heroin dependency was a matter of national interest and so beyond the
power of the provinces to address.

The Act did not create a new crime of narcotic dependency. The provisions of the
Act relating to the examination, apprehension and detention of dependent persons
were not intended to be punitive. The legislation sought to cure a medical condition rather than punish a criminal activity. It was not a colourable attempt to legislate in the field of criminal law.

The Act was held not to be within the scope of any federal power to legislate for
the implementation of international treaties. Canada was a party to the Single
Convention on Narcotic Drugs 1961, which provided for the treatment of drug addicts and for measures against the abuse of drugs. Under the treaty, Canada was
bound to involve itself in active treatment which it had failed to do. There was
nothing in the Narcotic Control Act to suggest that it was enacted pursuant to any
of Canada's treaty obligations.

The pith and substance of the Act was medical treatment of addicts and thus within
the legislative jurisdiction of the province under the subject of public health, as be-

ing a matter of a local or private nature in the province. There was no conflict between federal legislation controlling illicit narcotics and provincial legislation for the treatment of dependent persons.

RIGHTS AND FREEDOMS

Application of the Canadian Charter of Rights and Freedoms

119. Operation Dismantle v. The Queen
[1985] 1 S.C.R. 441, 13 C.C.R. 287

The federal Cabinet made a decision to allow the United States to test cruise missiles in Canada. The appellant, O, brought an action in Federal Court for a declaration that the Cabinet decision was unconstitutional, for an injunction, and for damages. The Crown sought to strike out the statement of claim as disclosing no cause of action. The trial judge dismissed the motion to strike, but the Court of Appeal allowed the appeal.

The Supreme Court of Canada held that the application of the Charter under s. 32(1)(a) to "the Parliament and government of Canada" extended to decisions of Cabinet. There was no reason to distinguish between Cabinet decisions made pursuant to statutory authority and those made in the exercise of the royal prerogative. Therefore, the decision was reviewable in the courts to determine whether or not it was compatible with the Constitution. Although it would have been difficult to determine whether or not testing would increase the risk of nuclear war, that difficulty did not affect the question of whether the Court had a duty to consider the matter. The Court was not being asked to comment on the soundness of the decision, it was being asked to determine whether the Charter applied, and so it had a duty to address the issue.

The decision in this case was not contrary to the duties of the executive under the Charter. O alleged that the decision to test the cruise missile would lead to an increased threat of nuclear war. Section 7 of the Charter did not impose on the government a duty to refrain from acts which might lead to the deprivation or threatened deprivation of life, liberty and security of the person. The speculative nature of the allegation led to the conclusion that there was no duty on the Canadian Government to refuse the testing. The appeal was dismissed.

120. *Retail, Wholesale and Department Store Union, Local 580 v. Dolphin Delivery Ltd.*
[1986] 2 S.C.R. 573, 25 C.R.R. 321

The appellant, R, was the bargaining agent under a federal certification for the employees of P, a courier company. The respondent, D, was a courier company who had done business with P before P locked out its employees. After the lock-out, D engaged in business with S, another courier company. R applied to the British Columbia Labour Relations Board for a declaration that D and S were allies of P in their labour dispute with the appellant, thereby allowing the picketing of D's place of business. The Board declined to make the order on the ground of lack of jurisdiction, holding that the relationship between R and P would be governed by the Canada Labour Code. Since the Canada Labour Code was silent on the issue, the matter fell to be determined under the common law.

R informed D that its place of business would be picketed unless it agreed to stop doing business with S. D applied for and was granted an injunction to restrain R from picketing its business premises.

On appeal to the Court of Appeal, R raised the issue that the granting of the injunction had the effect of infringing its freedom of expression and freedom of association under s. 2 of the Charter of Rights and Freedoms. A majority of the Court held that the activity being restrained could not be protected by invoking either freedom of expression or freedom of association. On appeal to the Supreme Court of Canada, the issue was confined to the allegation that the injunction infringed freedom of expression.

The Supreme Court observed that any form of picketing involved some element of expression. Protection of freedom of expression would not extend to protect acts or threats of violence, or other unlawful conduct. However, it was found in this case that the picketing would have been peaceful, and thus would have involved the right of freedom of expression.

The Court held that the Charter did apply to common law, but not to private litigation. In this case, in a dispute between private parties, an injunction was granted to prevent commission of the common law torts of civil conspiracy and inducement of breach of contract, where the injunction allegedly infringed the Charter right of freedom of expression. In order for the Charter to apply, it was necessary to have some sort of government intervention or intrusion, such as a statutory provision specifically outlawing secondary picketing of the type subject to the injunction. Since there was no such governmental action, the Charter did not apply and the appeal was dismissed.

121. *Borowski v. Canada (Attorney General)*
[1989] 1 S.C.R. 342, 51 D.L.R. (4th) 231

After the decision of *Minister of Justice of Canada and Minister of Finance of Canada v. Borowski (32)*, in which the appellant B was granted standing to bring an action to declare several sections of the Criminal Code invalid, he filed an amended statement of claim in which he repeated claims based on alleged violations of the Canadian Bill of Rights, and added claims based on alleged violations of the Charter. His action was dismissed at trial and on appeal.

B appealed on the issues of whether an unborn child had the right to life as guaranteed by s. 7 and the right to equal protection of the law as guaranteed by s. 15 of the Charter and, if so, whether the relevant sections of the Criminal Code denied those rights. After B obtained leave to appeal to the Supreme Court of Canada, the Court struck down the relevant sections of the Criminal Code in *R. v. Morgentaler (1988) (141)*. The Attorney General applied to adjourn the hearing, arguing that the Criminal Code issue was moot and the questions regarding the Charter were not severable. The application was denied, and the appeal proceeded.

The Supreme Court observed that a case would be moot in the absence of a "present live controversy". In this case the basis for B's action disappeared with the striking down of the various sections of the Criminal Code. The questions relating to the Charter were merely ancillary to the central issue of the alleged unconstitutionality of the Criminal Code provisions. The appeal was therefore moot, however the Court was entitled to exercise its discretion to decide the appeal on the merits.

The Court reviewed the three criteria of an adversarial context, a concern for judicial economy, and an awareness of the Court's adjudicative function in deciding not to exercise its discretion to hear the appeal on the merits.

On the issue of standing, the Court held that standing under the Charter could be gained either through s. 24 or s. 52. Section 24 allowed anyone whose rights had been infringed to apply for a remedy. B's claim did not meet this test as he did not allege a violation of his own rights. Section 52 was restricted to the challenge of a law or governmental action. The claim failed this requirement as well, since B sought a naked interpretation of two provisions of the Charter. For the Court to answer purely abstract questions would have been to sanction a private reference.

Since the action was moot and B lacked standing, the appeal was dismissed.

122. *McKinney v. University of Guelph*
[1990] 3 S.C.R. 229, 76 D.L.R. (4th) 545

The respondent, U, and other universities established policies which provided for the mandatory retirement of staff at age 65. M and the other appellants were employed by the various universities. The appellants applied for a declaration that the retirement policies violated s. 15 of the Charter by discriminating on the basis of age. They also sought a declaration that s. 15 of the Charter was violated by s. 9(*a*) of the Ontario Human Rights Code, which defined "age" for the purposes of employment as being between 18 years and 65 years.

The action was dismissed. The trial judge held that the Charter did not apply to the mandatory retirement policies of the universities. Section 9(*a*) of the Ontario Human Rights Code did offend s. 15 of the Charter, but it was held to be justified as a reasonable limit under s. 1. The Court of Appeal dismissed the appeal on the same grounds.

The Supreme Court of Canada dismissed the appeal. Speaking through La Forest J., three judges of seven held that the Charter was confined to government action. To hold otherwise would be to seriously diminish individual freedom of action. The appellants argued that universities were creatures of statute which exercised powers pursuant to statute and carried out public functions pursuant to statutory authority, and as such constituted part of the legislature or government of the province within the meaning of s. 32 of the Charter. It was acknowledged that universities were subjected to important limitations, either through regulation or government funding. However, the universities were autonomous in that the government had no legal power to control them. They did not form part of the government apparatus, so their actions did not fall within the ambit of the Charter. The mandatory retirement policy was not a government policy. Although the Charter did not apply, it was further held that the retirement policy would have been a violation of s. 15, but that it was justified under s. 1 as a reasonable limit. Section 9(*a*) of the Ontario Human Rights Code violated s. 15, but it too was justified as a reasonable limit.

In dissent, Wilson J. agreed that the Charter applied only to government action. However, she concluded that the mandatory retirement policies of the universities were subject to scrutiny under s. 15 of the Charter. The government exercised substantial control over the universities, education at every level has been a traditional function of governments in Canada, and each province was found to have a vital interest in a quality educational system. These three factors led to the conclusion that universities formed part of government for the purposes of s. 32 of the Charter. The policies did infringe s. 15 and could not be justified under s. 1. The same conclusion was reached in respect of s. 9(*a*) of the Ontario Human Rights Code.

Cory J. agreed with the reasons and conclusions of Wilson J. that universities form part of government for the purposes of s. 32 of the Charter. However, he agreed with La Forest J. that the retirement policies were justified under s. 1. Section 9(*a*) of the Ontario Human Rights Code infringed but was justified.

L'Heureux-Dubé J. in dissent held that the Charter did not apply to the mandatory retirement policies, but that s. 9(*a*) of the Ontario Human Rights Code did unjustifiably infringe the Charter.

123. *Harrison v. University of British Columbia*
[1990] 3 S.C.R. 451, 77 D.L.R. (4th) 55

Pursuant to the policy of the appellant, U, the respondent, H, and others were retired from their employment with the university at age 65. H applied for declarations that the mandatory retirementpolicy violated s. 15 of the Charter as discriminating on the basis of age. H also sought declarations that s. 15 of the Charter was violated by s. 1 of the Human Rights Act of British Columbia, which defined "age" for the purpose of employment discrimination as being between 45 years and 65 years.

The trial judge held that the Charter did not apply to the university's retirement policy. Further, the definition of age was a matter of legislative discretion and did not constitute age-based discrimination for those aged 65 and over. The Court of Appeal affirmed the holding that the Charter did not apply to the university. However, the appeal was allowed to the extent that the provisions of the Human Rights Code with respect to age did infringe s. 15(1) of the Charter and were not justified under s. 1 as a reasonable limit. U appealed with respect to the issues relating to the Human Rights Act. H cross-appealed on the issue of the application of the Charter to the mandatory retirement policy.

A majority of the Supreme Court of Canada allowed the appeal and dismissed the cross-appeal for the reasons given in *McKinney v. University of Guelph (121)*. Although there were facts suggesting a greater degree of governmental control in this case, the control was not at a level that would justify application of the Charter.

It was argued that the provisions of the Human Rights Code defining "age" constituted an affirmative action measure within the meaning of s. 15(2) of the Charter so as to exclude the operation of s. 15(1). The majority found it unnecessary to decide the issue. Wilson J. in dissent rejected the argument that older workers under the age of 65 were subject to discrimination by not being entitled to certain benefits available to those aged 65 and over. Older workers under age 65 did not suffer the burden of prejudice and stereotype by reason of being unable to enjoy such benefits. Therefore, there was no disadvantage of the type sought to be ameliorated by programs contemplated under s. 15(2). Wilson J. concluded that both the retirement policy and the provisions of the Human Rights Act infringed s. 15(1) and could not be saved under s. 1. She would have struck down the definition of "age" to the extent that it set an upper limit of 65 years.

L'Heureux-Dubé J. concluded that the Charter did not apply to U, but that the provisions of the Human Rights Act did violate s. 15(1) of the Charter and could not be justified under s. 1.

124. *Cuddy Chicks Ltd. v. Ontario (Labour Relations Board)*
[1991] 2 S.C.R. 5, 81 D.L.R. (4th) 121

A union filed an application for certification before the respondent, O, relating to employees at the chicken hatchery of the appellant, C. Section 2(*b*) of the Labour Relations Act provided that the Act did not apply to "a person employed in agriculture". The position of C was that their employees were agricultural employees. The union gave notice that if the employees were found to be agricultural employees, it would request O to hold s. 2(*b*) invalid as infringing freedom of association and equality rights under ss. 2(*d*) and 15 of the Charter. C disputed O's jurisdiction to entertain Charter issues.

O concluded that it did have jurisdiction to rule on Charter issues. That conclusion was affirmed by both the Divisional Court and the Court of Appeal. An appeal was taken to the Supreme Court of Canada on the issues of whether s. 52 of the Constitution Act conferred the right and duty on O to decide the constitutional validity of its enabling statute, whether O had jurisdiction by virtue of its duty to consider external statutes bearing on proceedings before it, and whether O was a "court of competent jurisdiction" under s. 24(1) of the Charter. The question of whether or not s. 2(*b*) of the Labour Relations Act infringed the Charter was not in issue.

The Supreme Court observed that s. 52(1) of the Constitution Act did not specifically confer jurisdiction on administrative tribunals. However, the principle of supremacy of the Constitution articulated in s. 52(1) led to the conclusion that any tribunal with the power to interpret law had a concomitant power to determine the constitutional validity of the law. The tribunal had to have jurisdiction over the whole of the matter before it: the parties, the subject matter, and the remedy. In this case O had jurisdiction over the parties. The question was whether it had jurisdiction over the subject matter and the remedy, both of which were premised on the application of the Charter. The source of the tribunal's jurisdiction was the tribunal's enabling statute, the Labour Relations Act, which stated that the board had exclusive jurisdiction "to determine all questions of fact or law that arise in any matter before it". Since a Charter issue was a question of law, O had authority to rule on the constitutionality of its enabling statute.

The Court went on to state that O could treat any impugned provision as invalid strictly for the purposes of the matter before it. As such, any decision of O would not be a binding legal precedent. The consideration of whether O was a court of competent jurisdiction was viewed as unnecessary. The appeal was dismissed.

See also *Lavigne v. Ontario Public Service Employees Union (138)*

Limitation of Rights and Freedoms

125. *R. v. Therens*
[1985] 1 S.C.R. 613, 13 C.C.R. 193

The respondent, T, lost control of the vehicle that he was driving, and as a result a police officer made a demand under s. 235 of the Criminal Code requiring T to accompany the officer for the purpose of obtaining samples of T's breath for analysis. T accompanied the officer and supplied breath samples, and was subsequently charged under s. 236(1) of the Criminal Code. T was never informed of his right to retain and instruct counsel, which was the basis of his application under s. 24 of the Charter to exclude evidence of the breathalyzer technician's certificate of analysis at his trial. The trial judge allowed the application, ordered the exclusion of the certificate, and dismissed the charge. The Court of Appeal dismissed the appeal.

In the Supreme Court of Canada, Le Dain J. extensively discussed the meaning of the word "detention" in the context of s. 10 of the Charter. The word referred to "a restraint of liberty other than arrest in which a person may reasonably require the assistance of counsel but might be prevented or impeded from retaining and instructing counsel without delay but for the constitutional guarantee." (at 642 S.C.R.) The definition contemplated both physical constraint and control over movement by demand or direction. In this case, since refusal to comply with a demand under s. 235 of the Criminal Code was an offence, that criminal liability constituted effective compulsion. In general, compliance with a demand from a police officer could not be considered voluntary since most people would not know the precise extent of police authority and would feel compelled to comply.

Having concluded that T had been detained within the meaning of s. 10 of the Charter, Le Dain J. went on to consider whether the evidence should have been excluded. Evidence could be excluded only under s. 24(2), where to admit it would bring the administration of justice into disrepute. It could not be excluded under s. 24(1) simply on the basis that it would be appropriate and just in the circumstances to do so.

In applying s. 24(2), it was unnecessary to establish that the evidence would not have been obtained but for the Charter infringement. All that was necessary was that the infringement of the right precede the obtaining of the evidence. In this case the evidence was obtained in a manner that infringed T's right to be informed of his right to retain and instruct counsel without delay.

The denial of right to counsel was seen to be of such fundamental importance as to *prima facie* discredit the administration of justice. However, under the state of the law at the time of arrest, the police officer was found to be entitled to assume in good faith that T was not being detained and thus did not have a right to counsel on demand. Therefore, the admission of the evidence would not bring the administration of justice into disrepute and the evidence could not be excluded.

The rest of the Court agreed that T had been detained, and that T's rights under s. 10 of the Charter had been violated. Five judges agreed that the admissibility of evidence fell to be determined under s. 24(2) and not s. 24(1). Dickson C.J. and Lamer J. agreed that s. 24(2) applied, but chose not to decide the applicability of s. 24(1). However, the majority of the Court disagreed with the conclusion of Le Dain J. that the evidence not be excluded. Exclusion of the evidence would have invited police officers to disregard the rights of citizens with an assurance of impunity. The appeal was dismissed.

126. *Singh v. Minister of Employment and Immigration*
[1985] 1 S.C.R. 177, 14 C.R.R. 13

S and six other appellants asserted claims to Convention refugee status under the Immigration Act. The respondent, M, determined that none of the appellants was a Convention refugee. The appellants applied for redetermination of status by the Immigration Appeal Board (the "Board"), but the Board held that there were no reasonable grounds to believe that a claim could be established and refused the applications. Applications for judicial review of the Board's decision were denied by the Federal Court of Appeal.

On appeal to the Supreme Court of Canada, the appellants contended that they did not have a fair opportunity to present their refugee status claims or to know the case they had to meet. They alleged that the procedures set out in the Immigration Act denied their right to life, liberty and security of the person under s. 7 of the Canadian Charter of Rights and Freedoms. Six judges of a seven-member panel took part in the judgment.

Three of the judges held that the word "everyone" in s. 7 included every human being physically present in Canada who, by virtue of such presence, were amenable to Canadian law. M conceded that the appellants were included in the definition but did not concede that the rights asserted by the appellants fell within s. 7. Under the Immigration Act, a Convention refugee had the right to a determination as to whether a permit should be issued to entitle entry to Canada, the right not to be returned to a country where life or freedom would be threatened, and the right to appeal a removal order or a deportation order. Denial of these rights was held to be a deprivation of the right to life, liberty and security of the person.

Immigration Act procedures did not allow adequate opportunity to state the claimant's case, or to allow the claimant to know the Minister's case that had to be met. Such procedures did not accord the refugee claimants fundamental justice and thus infringed s. 7 of the Charter. M failed to demonstrate that the procedures constituted a reasonable limit on the appellants' rights, so the provisions could not be saved under s. 1.

The other three judges decided the appeal on the basis of the Canadian Bill of Rights, which was left operational by the Charter. It was held that the appellants were not afforded a fair hearing in accordance with the principles of fundamental justice within the meaning of s. 2(e) of the Bill of Rights.

The appeals were allowed, the decisions of the Federal Court of Appeal and the Immigration Appeal Board set aside, and the cases were remanded to the Board for hearing on the merits in accordance with the principles of fundamental justice.

127. *R. v. Oakes*
[1986] 1 S.C.R. 103, 19 C.R.R. 308

The respondent, O, was charged with trafficking in narcotics. The Crown relied on s. 8 of the Narcotic Control Act, which required the accused to prove that possession of a narcotic was not for the purpose of trafficking. The trial judge acquitted on the ground that the reverse onus provision infringed the right to presumption of innocence under s. 11(d) of the Charter. The Court of Appeal dismissed the appeal.

The Supreme Court of Canada agreed that the reverse onus provision violated the presumption of innocence, even though the standard of proof was on a balance of probabilities. If an accused adduced sufficient evidence to raise a reasonable doubt as to innocence but did not prove on a balance of probabilities that the presumed fact was untrue, the accused could be convicted despite the existence of a reasonable doubt.

The Court observed that the onus of proving a reasonable and demonstrably justified limit under s. 1 of the Charter was on the party seeking to uphold the limit. The standard of proof was the civil standard, as the criminal standard was unduly onerous in the context of the words used s. 1. It was necessary to show that the objective of the limitation was of sufficient importance to warrant overriding a constitutionally protected right or freedom. Once that was established, it was necessary to invoke a "proportionality test" to show that the means chosen were reasonable.

The proportionality test involved three components. First, the measures adopted to achieve the limitation had to be carefully designed so as to be rationally connected to the objective. Second, the measures had to impair as little as possible the right or freedom in question. Third, there had to be a proportionality between the effects of the measures and the objective identified as being of sufficient importance to override the constitutional right or freedom.

Section 8 of the Narcotic Control Act was aimed at curbing drug trafficking. That objective was viewed as being of sufficient importance to warrant overriding a constitutionally protected right or freedom. However, the mere fact of possession of a small quantity of narcotics did not support the inference that the accused intended to engage in trafficking. Therefore, there was no rational connection between the measures and the objective. Section 8 did not meet the first part of the proportionality test and as such could not be justified under s. 1. The appeal was dismissed.

128. *R. v. Chaulk*
[1990] 3 S.C.R. 1303, 1 C.R.R. (2d) 1

The appellants, C and another, were youths who confessed to entering a house and killing the occupant. At trial, their defence of insanity was rejected and they were convicted of first degree murder. They appealed on the ground that s. 16(4) of the Criminal Code was unconstitutional. Section 16(4) provided that everyone was to be presumed sane in the absence of proof to the contrary. The appeal was dismissed. A further appeal was taken to the Supreme Court of Canada on the issue of whether s. 16(4) was inconsistent with the presumption of innocence under s. 11(*d*) of the Charter.

In the Supreme Court the Crown argued that since insanity did not disprove an offence, the presumption of innocence did not apply to s. 16. This argument was rejected by Lamer J. If a provision required an accused to prove some fact on the balance of probabilities to avoid conviction, the provision violated the presumption of innocence because it permitted a conviction in spite of a reasonable doubt as to the accused's guilt. Sanity was an essential element of guilt. Section 16(4) allowed the fact of sanity to be presumed, rather than proven. Therefore, the provision violated the presumption of innocence under the Charter.

It was further argued that the verdict of not guilty by reason of insanity was not a determination of guilt or innocence, so the presumption of innocence did not apply. However, such a verdict was held to be a determination of criminal responsibility, and therefore the presumption of innocence did apply.

The objective of s. 16(4) was to avoid placing on the Crown the "impossibly onerous burden" (Whyte, Lederman & Bur, p. 19-57) of disproving insanity and thereby secure the conviction of the guilty. This objective was sufficiently important to warrant an infringement of constitutionally protected rights. There was a rational connection between the objective and the provision in question. It was possible to imagine scenarios which impaired an accused's rights to a lesser extent than s. 16(4), but the Court was not to second-guess the legislators. Parliament might not have chosen the least intrusive means of meeting its objective, but it chose from a range of means impairing s. 11(*d*) as little as possible. Section 16(4) represented an accommodation of the societal interests of avoiding an impossible evidentiary burden on the Crown, convicting the guilty, and acquitting those who lack capacity. The resulting compromise led to the conclusion that there was proportionality between the effects of the measure and its objective. Therefore, the infringement was a reasonable limit under s. 1. The appeal was allowed on other grounds and a new trial ordered.

Sopinka J. agreed with Lamer J. as to the constitutional questions but dismissed the appeal. Gonthier J. disagreed with Lamer J. as to the constitutional questions but allowed the appeal. McLachlin J. held that the provision was not inconsistent with the Charter and dismissed the appeal. Wilson J. held that the provision was inconsistent with the Charter and not justified under s. 1.

129. *R. v. Keegstra*
[1990] 3 S.C.R. 697, 3 C.R.R. (2d) 193

The respondent, K, was a high school teacher. As a result of comments made to his students about Jews and the Holocaust, he was charged under s. 319(2) of the Criminal Code with promoting hatred against an identifiable group. He was convicted at trial but his appeal was allowed by the Alberta Court of Appeal.

An appeal was taken to the Supreme Court of Canada on the issues of whether s. 319(2) infringed on freedom of expression under s. 2(*b*) of the Charter, and whether s. 319(3) infringed the presumption of innocence under s. 11(*d*). Section 319(3) provided that an accused could defend a charge under s. 319(2) by proving the truth of the communicated statement.

A majority of the Supreme Court held that in assessing infringement of freedom of expression, "expression" was defined as embracing all content of expression regardless of the meaning or message conveyed. K's activities had an expressive content intended to be restricted by the provisions of the Criminal Code. Section 319(2) therefore violated the right to freedom of expression.

In assessing whether s. 319(2) could be justified as a reasonable limit, the majority concluded that the objective of the section in curbing the harm flowing from hate propaganda was of the utmost importance. Thus there was a powerfully convincing legislative objective to justify limits on freedom of expression.

In applying the proportionality test, it was held that the suppression of hate propaganda reduced the harm done to the targeted individuals and to the relations between various cultural groups. Therefore, the means chosen to further the purpose of the legislation were held to be rational. Section 319(2) possessed a stringent *mens rea* requirement; it excluded private conversation, and it confined the definition of the offence to communication directed at an identifiable group. Therefore, it did not unduly impair freedom of expression. Promotion of hatred of identifiable groups was found to be of limited importance when measured against free expression values. Therefore, the provision satisfied all three components of the proportionality inquiry set out in *R. v. Oakes (127)*, and the infringement on freedom of expression was justified under s. 1.

The majority also found that s. 319(3) violated the presumption of innocence. The reverse onus provision was seen to be rationally connected to the valid objective of eliminating the wilful promotion of hatred. The requirement on the accused to prove truthfulness on a balance of probabilities was a valid precaution against too easily justifying the harm caused by the promotion of hatred, and thus a minimal impairment on the presumption of innocence. The importance of preventing the harm was not outweighed by the infringement of freedom of expression. The section was therefore justified under s. 1 of the Charter. The appeal was allowed.

The dissenting judges held that the provisions were inappropriate, citing as reasons the breadth of category of speech affected, the absolute prohibition involved, the draconian criminal consequences, the availability of alternate remedies, and the counterproductive nature of the effects of the legislation.

See also *Edwards Books and Art Ltd. v. The Queen (131)* and *McKinney v. University of Guelph (122)*

Legislative Override

130. *Ford v. Quebec (Attorney General)*
[1988] 2 S.C.R. 712, 36 C.R.R. 1

Section 58 of the Quebec Charter of the French Language required public signs and posters and commercial advertising to be in French only. Section 69 of the language Charter allowed only the French version of a firm name to be used. The respondents, F and others, put up advertising signs that were in both English and French. They were informed that the signs did not conform with the language Charter and were asked to alter them. Some of the respondents were charged with violation of the language Charter. They brought an action for a declaration that ss. 58 and 69 were inoperative. At trial, s. 58 was declared inoperative as infringing freedom of expression under the Quebec Charter of Human Rights and Freedoms. The Court of Appeal declared both ss. 58 and 69 to be inoperative, because of both the Quebec Charter of Rights and the Canadian Charter of Rights.

Section 33(1) of the Canadian Charter of Rights provided for Parliament or a legislature expressly to declare a statute to operate notwithstanding any provision included in s. 2 or ss. 7 to 15. Pursuant to s. 33(1), the Quebec Legislature enacted legislation declaring all provincial laws to operate notwithstanding those Charter provisions. The legislative override provision of the Act to Amend the Charter of the French Language was s. 52. An appeal was taken to the Supreme Court of Canada on the issues of whether s. 52 was inconsistent with s. 33(1) of the Canadian Charter of Rights and, if so, whether ss. 58 and 69 of the language Charter and their corresponding penalty provisions offended freedom of expression under s. 2(*b*) of the Canadian Charter of Rights and Freedoms.

The Supreme Court held a s. 33 override declaration to be sufficiently express if it referred to the number of the section, subsection, or paragraph of the Charter containing the provision to be overridden. The Court rejected the argument that a s. 33 declaration had to specify the actual guarantee sought to be overridden. Therefore, s. 52 of the Act to Amend the Charter of the French Language was a sufficient legislative override to protect s. 58 from the s. 2(*b*) guarantee of freedom of expression. Section 69 was found not to have been affected by the Act to Amend the French Language, and was therefore not protected from the operation of s. 2(*b*) of the Canadian Charter.

Since the Charter required a large and liberal interpretation, there was no sound basis on which commercial expression could be excluded from the s. 2(*b*) guarantee of freedom of expression. Language was so intimately related to the form and content of expression that there could be no true freedom of expression by means of language if there were a prohibition on using the language of one's choice. Therefore, the s. 2(*b*) freedom of expression included the freedom of expression in the language of one's choice. Section 69 therefore infringed s. 2(*b*). Section 58 which was protected from s. 2(*b*), was found to have breached the freedom of expression guarantee under the Quebec Charter of Rights.

Freedom of Religion

131. *Edwards Books and Art Ltd. v. The Queen*
[1986] 2 S.C.R. 713, 28 C.R.R. 1

The appellants, E and several other retailers, were charged with failing to ensure that no goods were sold or offered for sale by retail on a holiday contrary to s. 2 of the Retail Business Holidays Act (the "Act"). Each of the appellants admitted to having a store open for business on a Sunday. One of the retailers observed a Saturday Sabbath and was acquitted; the others were convicted. An appeal was taken to the Supreme Court of Canada on the issues of whether the Act was *intra vires* the provincial legislature under s. 92 of the British North America Act, and whether the Act infringed religious freedom under s. 2(*a*) of the Canadian Charter of Rights and Freedoms.

Speaking for three judges, Dickson C.J. held that the purpose of the Retail Business Holidays Act was to provide uniform holidays to retail workers. The Act included secular holidays and provided exemptions pertaining to small businesses and tourism, suggesting that it was motivated by secular and not religious values. Therefore, it was valid legislation in relation to property and civil rights and not a colourable scheme to promote or prefer religious observance.

Section 3(4) of the Act permitted limited opening on Sunday for retailers closed the previous Saturday. However, this exemption was open to retailers of any religion. It was a valid attempt, in the context of otherwise valid provincial legislation, to attempt to minimize or neutralize the adverse effects of the legislation on freedom of religion. Therefore, neither the Act nor the exemption were *ultra vires*.

The same observations regarding legislative purpose applied to the arguments raised under the Charter. The secular purpose of the Act did not offend freedom of religion under s. 2(*a*) merely because the statutory provisions coincided with the tenets of a particular religion. However, in assessing the impact of the Act, it was observed that those who observed a day of rest on Saturday suffered a competitive disadvantage at the hands of those observing a day of rest on Sunday. Therefore, the Act abridged freedom of religion. However, it was found to be justified under s. 1.

Speaking for two judges, Beetz J. held that any economic harm suffered by a retailer closing shop on a Saturday to observe a day of rest was not caused by the Act, but by a deliberate choice to give priority to religion over financial benefit. The Act therefore did not violate freedom of religion.

La Forest J. wrote an opinion largely concurring with that of Dickson C.J., focusing on the nature of the exemptions to Sunday observance.

Wilson J. agreed that the Act infringed freedom of religion. However, s. 3(4) created an exemption only for retailers operating with no more than seven employees or 5,000 square feet of floor space. Therefore the exemption did not recognize the religious freedom of all members of a particular group and thus was not justifiable under s. 1.

The appeals from the convictions were dismissed and the Crown's appeal of the acquittal was allowed.

See also *R. v. Big M Drug Mart Ltd. (26)*

Freedom of Expression

132. *Reference re ss. 193 and 195.1(1)(c) of the Criminal Code (Prostitution Reference)*
[1990] 1 S.C.R. 1123, 56 C.C.C. (3d) 65

Section 193 of the Criminal Code prohibited the keeping of a bawdy house and made it an offence to be in a bawdy house. Section 195.1(1)(c) made it an offence to communicate with anyone in a public place for the purposes of obtaining the sexual services of a prostitute. The Lieutenant-Governor-in-Council of Manitoba referred questions to the Manitoba Court of Appeal to determine whether the two sections violated s. 2(*b*) or s. 7 of the Canadian Charter of Rights and Freedoms. The Court of Appeal held that there was no infringement.

Six judges of a seven-member panel of the Supreme Court of Canada participated in the decision. On behalf of three judges, Dickson C.J. held that s. 195.1 infringed s. 2(*b*) whereas s. 193 did not. The infringement by s. 195.1 was justified as a reasonable limit under s. 1. The objective of the legislation was to eradicate various forms of social nuisance arising from the public display of the sale of sex. This was a valid objective. There was a rational connection between the measure and the objective in that prohibiting the prostitute from soliciting and prohibiting the customer from propositioning in public places would prevent the public nuisance. Communication regarding an economic transaction of sex for money did not lie at or near the core guarantee of freedom of expression. The legislation was not unduly intrusive in its attempts to curtail visible solicitation. The decrease in social nuisance associated with street solicitation outweighed the obtrusiveness of the enforcement of the provision. Therefore, it was justified under s. 1 of the Charter.

With respect to s. 7, ss. 193 and 195 clearly infringed the right to liberty given the possibility of imprisonment. The provisions were not void for vagueness such that they did not comply with the principles of fundamental justice. Further, the fact that both communication and sale of sex for money were both legal activities did not impede Parliament's capacity to control street solicitation. Therefore, there was no violation of the principles of fundamental justice.

For two judges, Wilson J. held that s. 193 did not infringe the right to freedom of expression. However, s. 195.1 did infringe and was not justified as it did not meet the proportionality test. It was not reasonable to prohibit all expressive activity conveying a certain meaning taking place in public simply because in some circumstances and in some areas the activity might have given rise to a public or social nuisance. Further, s. 195.1 infringed the right to liberty because of a possible prison sentence and this was not a proportionate way of dealing with the public or social nuisance. Section 195.1 violated s. 7 of the Charter and was not saved by s. 1.

Lamer J. held that rights under s. 7 did not extend to the right to exercise a chosen profession and that therefore ss. 193 and 195.1 of the Criminal Code offended s. 7. Freedom of expression under s. 2(*b*) was infringed, but was justified under s. 1.

133. *Rocket v. Royal College of Dental Surgeons of Ontario*
   [1990] 2 S.C.R. 232, 47 C.R.R. 193

The respondents, R and another, were dentists. They were prominently featured in a newspaper and magazine advertisement for Holiday Inn. The advertisement mentioned the two respondents, described the success of their dental practice, and stated that when they travel they stay at the Holiday Inn. They were charged under s. 37(39) of Regulation 447 made under the Health Disciplines Act which placed restrictions on advertising. The respondents brought an action to challenge the constitutionality of the provision. The application was dismissed but the decision was reversed by the Court of Appeal.

The Supreme Court of Canada held that since professional advertising intends to convey a meaning, it constitutes expressive activity within the meaning of s. 2(*b*) of the Canadian Charter of Rights and Freedoms. In this case there was nothing offensive about the form of advertising, so it could not be excluded from the operation of s. 2(*b*) on the ground that it took a prohibited form. The purpose of s. 37(39) was to restrict both the content and the form of advertising by dentists. Therefore, the section prohibited legitimate forms of expression and purposefully limited the content of the expression so as to infringe s. 2(*b*).

The Court acknowledged the importance of allowing professional societies to regulate the conduct of their members, including the means by which they advertise. The regulation of advertising was required to maintain a high standard of professionalism, and to protect the public from irresponsible and misleading advertising. Therefore, the objective of the legislation in question was sufficiently important to warrant overriding a constitutionally protected right.

The first requirement of the proportionality test was met, in that the legislation was rationally connected to the objectives of promoting professionalism and avoiding irresponsible advertising. However, there was no proportionality found between the effect of the legislation and its objective. The section prohibited, without justification, the advertising of such useful and relevant information as office hours. As such the adverse effect of the infringement of free expression outweighed the benefits of s. 37(39), and the section was not justifiable under s. 1 of the Charter. The provision was struck down and the appeal was dismissed.

134. *Committee for the Commonwealth of Canada v. Canada*
[1991] 1 S.C.R. 139, 77 D.L.R. (4th) 385

The secretary and vice-president of the respondents CCC went to the Montreal International Airport to recruit members and to promote knowledge of their group by displaying placards and distributing leaflets. Such activities were prohibited by the Government Airport Concession Operations Regulations. The respondents brought an action in the Federal Court for declarations that the airport management had not respected their fundamental freedoms, and that the airport constituted a public forum where such freedoms could be exercised. The declarations were granted and an appeal to the Federal Court of Appeal was dismissed. An appeal was brought to the Supreme Court of Canada on the issue of whether the Government Airport Concession Operations Regulations infringed s. 2(*b*) of the Canadian Charter of Rights and Freedoms.

Lamer C.J. and Sopinka J. compared the interests of the individuals wishing to express themselves in a place owned by the government with the interests of the government in operating such a place. A government-owned place will often have a large number of people using it, which is suited to the individual's interest to have a wide audience. However, the individual must respect the specific purposes for which all government property is used. Therefore, to allow the government to deliver services to society as a whole, the individual must show that the form of expression sought to be protected is compatible with the functions of the public place. In this case, distribution of pamphlets was held not to be incompatible with the airport's primary function of accommodating the needs of the travelling public. However, the policy of prohibiting promotional activities was not a limit prescribed by law such that an analysis under s. 1 of the Charter was necessary.

McLachlin J. observed that freedom of expression does not imply freedom of forum. Freedom of expression under s. 2(*b*) of the Charter involved a position between the two extremes of an individual right to use any and all government property for the purposes of expression subject to s. 1, and the absence of any individual rights to use any government property for public expression. The purpose of the government officials in prohibiting the respondents' activities was not to suppress particular content, but to prohibit all propaganda regardless of its content. The purpose of the respondents was to participate in social and political decision making, which was a purpose underlying the guarantee of free expression. Therefore, there was an infringement of s. 2(*b*). It was found not to be justified under s. 1.

L'Heureux-Dubé J. held that the government's invariable practice of prohibiting all means of expression constituted a restriction of freedom of expression within the meaning of s. 2(*b*). The government could not justify the restriction simply by asserting property rights or by claiming that the expression was unrelated to the airport's function. Any proposed restrictions as to time, place and manner would have to be reasonable in the circumstances. In this case the restriction was vague and too broad, and could not be justified under s. 1.

The other three judges concurred in dismissing the appeal.

135. *R. v. Butler*
[1992] 1 S.C.R. 452, 89 D.L.R. (4th) 449

The appellant, B, owned a video store from which he sold pornographic video tapes and magazines. He was charged under the Criminal Code with several counts of selling obscene material, possessing obscene material for the purpose of distribution and sale, and exposing obscene material to public view. The trial judge convicted on some counts, but acquitted on the majority of the counts. The Manitoba Court of Appeal entered convictions for all of the counts. An appeal was brought to the Supreme Court of Canada on the issue of whether the provision of the Criminal Code making it an offence to sell or possess obscene material violated freedom of expression under s. 2(*b*) of the Canadian Charter of Rights and Freedoms.

The Criminal Code defined as obscene any publication whose dominant characteristic was the undue exploitation of sex. The Supreme Court considered the word "undue" as it was defined in three tests: the "community standard of tolerance" test, the "degradation or dehumanization" test, and the "internal necessities" or "artistic defence" test. To establish a relationship among the three tests, the subject of pornography was divided into three categories: explicit sex with violence, explicit sex without violence but with degrading or dehumanizing treatment, and explicit sex without violence that was neither degrading nor dehumanizing. The first category would almost always constitute undue exploitation of sex. The second category could involve undueness if there were a substantial risk of harm. The third category was generally tolerated unless children were involved. That analysis involvedthe first two tests. The "internal necessities" test applied only if a work contained sexually explicit material that by itself would constitute the undue exploitation of sex.

On the subject of freedom of expression, the Supreme Court held that the Court of Appeal erred in deciding that the materials involved purely physical activity and did not convey meaning. The subject matter of the materials was physical but that did not mean that they did not convey or attempt to convey meaning. The materials did have expressive content which was protected by s. 2(*b*) of the Charter and violated by the provisions of the Criminal Code.

The objective of the Criminal Code provisions was not moral disapprobation but the avoidance of harm to society. It was held to be an objective sufficiently pressing and substantial to warrant some restriction on the full exercise of the right to freedom of expression. There was a rational connection between the criminal sanction and the objective, in that it was reasonable to presume that exposure to images bore a causal relationship to changes in attitudes and beliefs. The provisions did not proscribe nonviolent, nondegrading, sexually explicit erotica, nor did they proscribe materials with scientific, literary, or artistic merit. Therefore, the legislation was appropriately tailored in the context of the infringed right and there was minimal impairment. The kind of expression sought to be protected was far from the coreof the guarantee of the freedom of expression and was primarily economically motivated, whereas the objective of the legislation was of fundamental importance. As such, the restriction on freedom of expression did not outweigh the legislative objective. So, even though the provisions infringed s. 2(*b*) of the Charter, they were justified as a reasonable limit under s. 1.

See also *Irwin Toy Ltd. v. Quebec (Attorney General) (92)*; *Retail, Wholesale and Department Store Union, Local 580 v. Dolphin Delivery Ltd. (120)*; and *Ford v. Quebec (Attorney General) (130)*

Freedom of Association

136. *Alberta Union of Provincial Employees v. Alberta (Attorney General)*
(Reference re Public Service Employee Relations Act)
[1987] 1 S.C.R. 313, 28 C.R.R. 305

Three Alberta statutes, the Labour Relations Act, the Police Officers Collective Bargaining Act, and the Public Service Employee Relations Act, prohibited the use of lockouts and strikes and provided compulsory arbitration as a mechanism for the resolution of labour disputes. A reference was directed to the Court of Appeal of Alberta for an advisory opinion on whether the relevant provisions of those statutes infringed any provision of the Canadian Charter of Rights and Freedoms. It was alleged that the right to strike, while not explicitly stated in the Charter, was implied in the freedom of association in s. 2(*d*). The Court of Appeal held that none of the provisions was inconsistent with the Charter.

The Supreme Court of Canada dismissed the appeal. McIntyre J. observed that the purpose or value of freedom of association was to allow the attainment of individual goals through the exercise of individual rights, which would generally be impossible without the aid and cooperation of others. McIntyre J. canvassed several approaches in attempting to define freedom of expression, and concluded that the concept allowed the individual to do in concert with others that which could be lawfully done alone. Conversely, individuals and organizations had no right to do in concert that which was unlawful when done individually. Therefore, the Charter would protect only those collective activities that would have Charter protection when exercised by an individual. The fact of association itself would not confer additional rights on individuals, so an association would not acquire a constitutionally guaranteed freedom to do anything that was unlawful for an individual to do.

The right to strike was not explicitly protected under the Charter, so it could only receive Charter protection if it were an activity permitted by law to an individual. However, there did not exist an individual right to strike. Therefore, the concept of freedom of association did not contemplate the constitutional guarantee of a right to strike.

Le Dain J. wrote a concurring opinion for three members of the Court, saying that the rights to strike and to bargain collectively were creations of legislation as opposed to fundamental rights or freedoms. Therefore, the activities of striking and collective bargaining should be regulated by legislative policy rather than be constitutionally protected.

In dissent, Dickson C.J. and Wilson J. held that protection of associational interests of employees in the collective bargaining process required protection of their freedom to collectively withdraw their services, and that the relevant provisions did unjustifiably infringe freedom of association.

137. *R. v. Skinner*
[1990] 1 S.C.R. 1235, 48 C.R.R. 90

The respondent, S, was charged with communicating in a public place for the purpose of obtaining the sexual services of a prostitute, contrary to s. 195.1(1)(*c*) of the Criminal Code. S alleged that the provision violated the freedoms of expression and association guaranteed in ss. 2(*b*) and 2(*d*) of the Canadian Charter of Rights and Freedoms. He was convicted at trial but the Nova Scotia Court of Appeal allowed his appeal.

A majority of the Supreme Court held that the offer of a service by a prostitute and the request for service by a customer clearly fell beyond the ambit of any definition of freedom of association considered in *Alberta Union of Provincial Employees v. Alberta (Attorney General) (136)*. The essence of the impugned legislation was that it attacked expressive activity of a commercial nature; it did not attack associational conduct. The mere fact that the provision limited the possibility of commercial activities was not enough to show a *prima facie* interference with freedom of association.

The argument that s. 195.1(1)(*c*) infringed freedom of expression was answered by the reasons given in *Reference re ss. 193 and 195.1(1)(c) of the Criminal Code (132)*. The provision did infringe freedom of expression under s. 2(*b*) but was justified under s. 1. It did not infringe freedom of association under s. 2(*d*). The Crown's appeal was allowed and the conviction and sentence restored.

The dissenting judges did not view expressive conduct and associational conduct as mutually exclusive. The effect of s. 195.1(1)(*c*) was to restrict the circumstances in which a prostitute and potential customer could meet or associate with a view to negotiating the sale of sexual services. There was thus an infringement of freedom of association which could not be justified under s. 1 because of the overly expansive definition of what constituted a "public place" for the purposes of the section.

138. *Lavigne v. Ontario Public Service Employees Union*
[1991] 2 S.C.R. 211, 81 D.L.R. (4th) 545

The appellant, L, was a teaching master and a member of the academic staff bargaining unit represented by the respondent, O. L was not a member of the union but he was required to pay union dues under the College Collective Bargaining Act. The dues were paid into the general revenues of the union and could be used for any purpose contemplated by the union's constitution. L was opposed to the use of his dues to support certain causes and brought an action for a declaration that the relevant provisions of the Act violated his freedoms of expression and association under subss. 2(*b*) and (*d*) of the Charter. The trial judge declared that L's rights had been violated but the decision was set aside by the Court of Appeal.

An appeal was taken to the Supreme Court of Canada on the issues of whether the Charter applied in the circumstances and if so, whether L's rights under subss. 2(*b*) and (*d*) of the Charter had been infringed.

The Supreme Court unanimously agreed that the Charter applied. L was compelled to pay union dues by a collective agreement rather than by operation of legislation. However, the bargaining agent for the college employers was the Ontario Council of Regents for Colleges of Applied Arts and Technology, which was an emanation of government. The Council was a Crown agent, and its concession to include in the collective agreement the provision for compulsory payment of union dues was government conduct.

A majority of the Court held that the provisions did not infringe L's freedom of association. Freedom of association was meant to protect the collective action of individuals in pursuit of common goals. L argued that s. 2(*d*) protected not only the right to associate, but also the right not to associate. However, that argument was interpreted as an extension of the right to associate, for which there was no compelling reason. A parallel was drawn with the mandatory payment of taxes, where s. 2(*d*) did not protect the ostensibly compelled associations with the policies of the political party in power. In this case, the payments could not reasonably be regarded as associating the individual with ideas and values to which the individual did not subscribe.

A minority of the Court held that freedom to associate and freedom not to associate were not distinct rights but rather two sides of a bilateral freedom whose purpose was the advancement of individual aspirations. In this case the financial contribution did constitute association. L's Charter rights had been infringed, but the infringement was found to be justified under s. 1.

The Court was unanimous in holding that compulsory payment of union dues was not an infringement of freedom of expression. The appeal was dismissed.

Life, Liberty and Security of the Person

139. *Reference re Section 94(2) of the Motor Vehicle Act*
[1985] 2 S.C.R. 486, 18 C.R.R. 30

Section 94(1) of British Columbia's Motor Vehicle Act made it an offence, punishable by fine and imprisonment, to drive while prohibited or suspended. Section 94(2) of the Act stated that s. 94(1) created an absolute liability offence in which guilt was established by proof of driving, regardless of whether or not the driver knew of the prohibition or suspension. A reference was brought to the British Columbia Court of Appeal to determine whether s. 94(2) was consistent with s. 7 of the Canadian Charter of Rights and Freedoms. The Court of Appeal held that it was not.

The Supreme Court of Canada unanimously dismissed the appeal. A majority of the Court interpreted the term "fundamental justice" in s. 7 not to be synonymous with the term "natural justice", for to do otherwise would have been unduly restrictive. The legal rights enumerated in ss. 8 to 14 of the Charter were viewed as specific deprivations of the right to life, liberty, and security of the person, such that s. 7 had to be interpreted at least as broadly as ss. 8 to 14. Further, ss. 8 to 14 illustrated the meaning of "principles of fundamental justice" by representing some of the essential elements of a system for the administration of justice.

The principle that the innocent not be punished was identified as one such essential element of a system for the administration of justice. The concept of absolute liability, to the extent that it had the potential to deprive life, liberty or security of the person, offended that principle. In this case the Act provided for imprisonment, which deprived liberty and thus infringed s. 7 of the Charter. The infringement could not be justified as a reasonable limit under s. 1, since the benefit of punishing bad drivers and removing them from the road did not outweigh the risk of imprisoning innocent people.

Wilson J. agreed with the conclusion that s. 94(2) unjustifiably infringed s. 7, but disagreed with the means by which ss. 8 to 14 were used to interpret the meaning of "fundamental justice". The penalty of mandatory imprisonment was totally disproportionate to the offence and thus offended the principles of fundamental justice.

140. *R. v. Vaillancourt*
[1987] 2 S.C.R. 636, 32 C.R.R. 18

The appellant, V, and his accomplice committed an armed robbery in a pool hall. V was armed with a knife and the accomplice with a gun. V's testimony was that he thought the gun was not loaded because he had seen his accomplice remove bullets from it. However, the victim died from gunshot wounds inflicted by the accomplice. V was a party to the offence committed by the accomplice by operation of s. 21(2) of the Criminal Code. V was convicted of second degree murder, and his conviction was upheld by the Quebec Court of Appeal.

An appeal was taken to the Supreme Court of Canada on the issue of whether s. 213(*d*) of the Criminal Code was inconsistent with either s. 7 or s. 11(*d*) of the Canadian Charter of Rights and Freedoms. Under section 213(*d*), a person using a weapon resulting in death while committing robbery was guilty of murder, regardless of whether the person intended to cause death or knew that death was likely to result.

V argued that according to the principles of fundamental justice, no criminal liability could be imposed for causing a particular result without some degree of subjective *mens rea*. A majority of the Court observed that the punishment and the social stigma attached to a conviction for murder were severe. Therefore, there had to be a special mental element giving rise to moral blameworthiness justifying the severity of the punishment and the stigma. A conviction could not rest on anything less than proof beyond a reasonable doubt of subjective foresight. For the purposes of this case, there could be no conviction in the absence of proof beyond a reasonable doubt of at least objective foreseeability.

The presumption of innocence in s. 11(*d*) of the Charter required proof beyond a reasonable doubt of the existence of all the essential elements of an offence. In this case, there could have been proof beyond a reasonable doubt that V carried the weapon during the commission of the offence, but there may have been reasonable doubt as to objective foreseeability of the likelihood of death being caused. Section 213 allowed a conviction in the absence of proof beyond a reasonable doubt of the essential element of objective foreseeability, and so violated ss. 7 and 11(*d*).

The objective of deterring the use or carrying of a weapon in the commission of certain offences was sufficiently important to warrant infringement of protected rights, and the means were rationally connected to that objective. However, in some instances the crime of carrying or using weapons was stigmatized as murder and therefore the Criminal Code provisions unduly impaired the rights and freedoms in question. Therefore, s. 213(*d*) violated both ss. 7 and 11(*d*) and was declared to be of no force and effect. The conviction was set aside and a new trial ordered.

In dissent, McIntyre J. held that while it may be illogical to characterize an unintentional killing as murder, it offended no principle of fundamental justice to classify as murder a serious criminal conduct involving the commission of a crime of violence resulting in death.

141. *R. v. Morgentaler (1988)*
[1988] 1 S.C.R. 30, 44 D.L.R. (4th) 385

The appellants, M and two others, were duly qualified medical practitioners who set up a clinic in Toronto to perform abortions. The clinic was not an accredited hospital within the meaning of s. 251(4) of the Criminal Code. That provision made it an offence to procure a miscarriage other than in an accredited hospital and without the approval of a therapeutic abortion committee.

The appellants moved to quash the indictments preferred against them or to stay the proceedings by challenging the constitutional validity of s. 251. The motion was dismissed, as was an appeal. The appellants were acquitted at trial, but a new trial was ordered by the Court of Appeal. An appeal was brought to the Supreme Court of Canada, principally on the issue of whether s. 251 infringed the right to life, liberty and security of the person under s. 7 of the Charter.

Dickson C.J. and Lamer J. concluded that s. 251 forced every pregnant woman to carry a foetus to term unless she could meet certain criteria unrelated to her own priorities and aspirations. This was held to be a profound interference with a woman's body such that it violated security of the person. The interference was aggravated by potential physical and emotional stress resulting from delays inherent in the administrative procedures prescribed by the section.

Beetz and Estey JJ. held that "security of the person" must include a right of access to medical treatment for a condition threatening life or health without fear of criminal consequences. The provision in this case potentially forced a choice between the commission of a crime to obtain timely and effective medical treatment, and inadequate treatment or no treatment at all. It therefore violated the right to security of the person.

Wilson J. held that the right to liberty gives a woman the right to decide for herself whether or not to terminate her pregnancy, and that s. 251 violated that right. Also, the effect of the section was to subject to state control the woman's capacity to reproduce, which was a direct interference with security of the person.

In dissent, McIntyre and La Forest JJ. held that apart from the therapeutic abortion provisions of the Criminal Code, no right of abortion was found in any Canadian law, custom or tradition. The Charter itself created no right to abortion. Therefore, s. 251 did not violate the right to security of the person.

A majority of the Court concluded that s. 251 of the Criminal Code infringed s. 7 of the Charter and was struck down in its entirety.

142. *R. v. Seaboyer; R. v. Gayme*
[1991] 2 S.C.R. 577, 83 D.L.R. (4th) 193

The respondents, S and G, had been charged and tried separately for sexual assault. At their respective preliminary inquiries both of them were prevented from cross-examining the complainant on prior sexual conduct. Section 276 of the Criminal Code prevented an accused from adducing evidence concerning the sexual activity of the complainant with someone other than the accused. Section 277 rendered inadmissible any evidence of sexual reputation for the purpose of challenging or supporting the credibility of the complainant. The respondents contended that the legislation infringed their right under s. 7 of the Canadian Charter of Rights and Freedoms not to be deprived of life, liberty and security of the person except in accordance with the principles of fundamental justice. There was also an argument that the sections violated the presumption of innocence under s. 11(*d*).

The respondents applied to the Supreme Court of Ontario for orders quashing the committals for trial on the ground that there was no opportunity to make full answer and defence. The orders were granted but the decision was reversed by the Ontario Court of Appeal. However, the court did not strike down ss. 276 and 277.

The Supreme Court of Canada acknowledged that the Criminal Code provisions did have the capacity to deprive the respondents of their liberty, so the question in issue was whether or not the deprivation was in accordance with the principles of fundamental justice.

The Crown contended that the purpose of the legislation was to abolish old common law rules admitting prejudicial evidence of little or no probative value, to encourage reporting of crime, and to protect the privacy of a witness. The defence acknowledged the legitimate purposes of the legislation, but contended that its effect was to interfere with the presentation of relevant evidence and thereby to violate the right to a fair trial.

With respect to s. 277, the Supreme Court held that the evidence sought to be excluded had no probative value and could serve no legitimate purpose in a trial. Therefore, the section did not infringe the right to a fair trial.

With respect to s. 276, the Court acceded to the argument of the defence, citing several examples of evidence of sexual conduct of probative value that would have been excluded under the provision. The section's blanket exclusion of all such evidence was overreaching in its attempt to fulfil the three stated objectives.

The trier of fact was prohibited from weighing the possible prejudicial effect of the evidence against its probative value. To encourage the reporting of crime by applying a rule which impaired the ability of the trier of fact to determine the truth was counterproductive. And, the right to a fair trial took precedence over protection of witness privacy. Underlying the right to a fair trial was the presumption of innocence expressed in s. 11(*d*). The blanket exclusion did not recognize individual circumstances, therefore s. 276 did infringe the respondents' rights.

The legislation did address a pressing and substantial objective, but it did not meet the proportionality test. Although there was arguably a rational connection between the measures and the purpose, the degree of impairment of the right was not appropriately restrained. The section did exclude irrelevant prejudicial evidence, but at the same time possibly excluded relevant evidence whose value was not outweighed by possible prejudicial effects. The section was therefore not saved by s. 1 of the Charter.

The striking down of the legislation did not revive the common law rules. Those rules did not conform to current reality so, like other common law rules, they had to be adapted to reflect that reality. The effect was to admit relevant evidence and exclude irrelevant evidence, subject to the qualification that the value of the evidence outweigh its potential prejudice to the conduct of a fair trial.

143. *Rodriguez v. British Columbia (Attorney General)*
[1993] 3 S.C.R. 519, 107 D.L.R. (4th) 342

The appellant, R suffered from amyotrophic lateral sclerosis. Her life expectancy was between two and 14 months. Her condition was deteriorating rapidly to the point where she would be unable to speak or care for herself. She was aware of her condition and the prognosis. She wished to control the circumstances, timing and manner of her death, but she would have been physically unable to take her own life without assistance. She wished to have a qualified medical practitioner set up the means by which she could take her own life at the time of her choosing. Section 241(*b*) of the Criminal Code made it an offence to counsel, aid or abet a person to commit suicide. R sought an order declaring that section invalid as violating her rights under ss. 7, 12, and 15 of the Canadian Charter of Rights and Freedoms.

The application was denied by the trial judge, and her appeal was dismissed by the British Columbia Court of Appeal. An appeal was brought to the Supreme Court of Canada on the issue of whether s. 241(*b*) infringed any of the rights guaranteed by the Charter.

A majority of the Court held that s. 241(*b*) did impinge on R's security, but any deprivation was not contrary to the principles of fundamental justice. Further, any consideration of the right to liberty and security could not be divorced from the sanctity of life. Canada and other Western countries recognized and applied the principle of sanctity of life as a general principle subject to limited and narrow exceptions involving notions of personal autonomy and dignity. However, for terminally ill persons, there was a distinction between withdrawing treatment upon a patient's request and active assisted suicide. There existed a general consensus that human life must be respected. Beyond that, there was little evidence of anything resembling a consensus with respect to the issue, and as such no evidence of violation of principles of fundamental justice, which would have to have general acceptance.

Mere prohibition by the state of a certain action was not "treatment", such that there was no violation of the s. 12 right to be free from cruel or unusual treatment or punishment. The majority assumed that equality rights under s. 15 were infringed, but were justified under s. 1.

McLachlin J. in dissent held that a legislative scheme limiting the rights of a person to deal with her body as she chooses may violate the principles of fundamental justice if the limit is arbitrary. Under the Criminal Code, assisted suicide was criminal whereas suicide was not. This was an arbitrary distinction. Section 7 was therefore breached and not found to be justified.

Lamer C.J. did not address the issues raised under ss. 7 and 12. Section 241(*b*) violated s. 15 equality rights by discriminating against persons unable to commit suicide by themselves.

Equality Rights

144. *Andrews v. Law Society of British Columbia*
[1989] 1 S.C.R. 143, 36 C.R.R. 193

The respondent, A, was a British subject permanently resident in Canada. The fact that he was not a Canadian citizen prevented him from being called to the Bar of British Columbia, for which he was otherwise qualified. He brought an action for a declaration that the section of the Law Society Act requiring Canadian citizenship violated the equality rights guaranteed under s. 15 of the Canadian Charter of Rights and Freedoms. The action was dismissed at trial but reversed on appeal.

A majority of the Supreme Court of Canada dismissed the Law Society's appeal. McIntyre and Lamer JJ. dissented, but the rest of the Court agreed with their approach to the interpretation of s. 15 of the Charter.

McIntyre J. wrote that s. 15 guaranteed equality in the application and formulation of the law, and did not guarantee equality in an abstract sense. The grounds of discrimination enumerated in s. 15 did not constitute an exhaustive list. Equality rights were to be determined not only by the enumerated grounds but by grounds considered to be analogous. However, not all grounds of distinction could be considered discriminatory. A complainant had to show that the impugned distinction had a discriminatory effect in the sense that it imposed burdens on an individual or group not imposed on others, or that it withheld advantages available to others, based on irrelevant personal differences. In this case, McIntyre J. held that the provision of the Law Society Act violated s. 15, but was sustainable under s. 1 achieving the goal of regulation and qualification of the legal profession.

The majority of the Court held that the Law Society Act violated the equality rights of non-citizens. Further, the relevant provision could not be justified under s. 1 because it did not meet the proportionality test. Although it was desirable for Canadian lawyers to be familiar with Canadian institutions and customs, the requirement of citizenship was not carefully tailored to achieve that objective. Citizenship did not ensure a commitment to the country or to the conscientious practice of law. Therefore, there was no rational connection between the measure and the objective.

145. *R. v. Turpin*
[1989] 1 S.C.R. 1296, 39 C.R.R. 306

The appellant, T, and two co-accused were charged in Ontario with first degree murder. Section 429 of the Criminal Code provided for a judge and jury to try indictable offences. T and the co-accused brought a motion to be tried by a judge alone, which was granted on the grounds that s. 11(*f*) of the Canadian Charter of Rights and Freedoms allowed the accused an election. Further, s. 430 of the Criminal Code provided for an election in the province of Alberta, but not in any of the other provinces. This was held to violate the equality provisions of s. 15 of the Charter. T was acquitted and the co-accused were convicted by a judge alone but the Court of Appeal ordered a new trial for first degree murder for all of them on the ground that the trial judge had no jurisdiction.

An appeal was brought to the Supreme Court of Canada on the issue of whether ss. 429 and 430 of the Criminal Code violated ss. 11(*f*) and 15 of the Charter.

The Supreme Court unanimously held that the impugned provisions denied the right to equality before the law. The accused were denied the opportunity to a trial by a judge alone, which was an opportunity available to those charged with the same offence in Alberta. The absence of choice was a disadvantage to the accused. However, even though there was denial of equality rights, there was no discrimination. Differentiating between Albertans and other Canadians for the purposes of trying indictable offences would not advance the purposes of s. 15 in remedying or preventing discrimination against groups suffering social, political and legal disadvantage in society. It therefore was not a fundamental principle of s. 15 that the criminal law apply equally throughout the country.

Section 11(*f*) of the Charter was held not to make obligatory a trial by jury. The accused was entitled to repudiate the right to trial by jury, as long as the repudiation was not in conflict with the mandatory jury trial provisions of the Criminal Code. The provisions did not violate s. 11(*f*). The appeal was dismissed.

146. *Egan v. Canada*
     Unreported, May 25, 1995 (S.C.C.), Doc. No. 23636, summarized at 95 C.L.L.C. 210-025

The appellants, E, cohabited in a homosexual relationship for many years. One of the appellants, upon attaining the age of 65 years, became eligible for old age security payments. His partner applied for a spousal allowance. The application was rejected on the basis that the appellants were not spouses within the meaning given by the Old Age Security Act, which defined a "spouse" in relation to any person as being of the opposite sex. The appellants brought an action in Federal Court for a declaration that the definition infringed the equality rights guaranteed in s. 15(1) of the Canadian Charter of Rights and Freedoms by discriminating on the basis of sexual orientation, and for a declaration that the definition be extended to same-sex partners. The Trial Division dismissed the claim and the decision was upheld by the Court of Appeal.

A majority of the Supreme Court of Canada dismissed the appeal. La Forest J. spoke for four judges in applying a three-step test of determining whether there was a distinction, whether the distinction resulted in a disadvantage, and whether the distinction was based on an irrelevant personal characteristic. It was clear that the Old Age Security Act made a distinction between the claimant in this case and others. The Crown conceded that protection of equality in s. 15 extended to sexual orientation. In assessing whether the distinction was based on an irrelevant personal characteristic, La Forest J. observed that marriage as a social institution was by nature heterosexual, in that heterosexual couples had the ability to procreate, that most children were the product of such relationships, and that the children were generally cared for by those living in such relationships. The same observations applied to unmarried heterosexual couples, which justified extending the definition of "spouse" in the Act to include those living in common-law relationships. The same observations did not apply to homosexual couples. Neither the purpose nor the effect of the legislation constituted an infringement of s. 15.

Cory, Iacobucci and McLachlin JJ. relied on ***Andrews v. Law Society of British Columbia (144)*** and ***R. v. Turpin (145)*** to apply a two-step test to determine whether s. 15 had been infringed. The first step involved an inquiry as to whether a distinction created by the impugned law denied to the claimant equality before the law, equality under the law, equal protection of the law or equal benefit of the law. In this case the Act denied equal benefit of the law by withholding from homosexual couples an economic benefit available to heterosexual couples. The second step involved determination of whether the distinction created by the law resulted in discrimination. The definition of "spouse" in the Act reinforced the stereotype that homosexuals did not form lasting and mutually supportive relationships with economic interdependence in the same manner as heterosexual couples. The legislation was therefore discriminatory and not justified under s. 1.

L'Heureux-Dubé J. agreed that the legislation did infringe s. 15 of the Charter and was not justified under s. 1, but applied the three-step approach of finding a legislative distinction, which led to a denial of equality rights, and was discriminatory. The concept of "discrimination" was to be first and foremost in the Court's analysis.

Sopinka J. agreed that the legislation did infringe s. 15 of the Charter, but held that it was justified under s. 1.

147. *Miron v. Trudel*
(1995), 23 O.R. (3d) 160*n*, [1995] I.L.R. 1-3185 (S.C.C.)

The appellants M and V were not married, but they lived together and had several children together. M was injured while a passenger in a vehicle driven by the respondent T. Neither T nor the owner of the vehicle was insured. As a result of the accident, M could not work. He made a claim for accident benefits for loss of income and damages against V's insurance policy, which extended accident benefits to the spouse of the policyholder. The insurance company denied the claim on the basis that M was not V's spouse as they were not legally married.

M and V sued the insurer, who brought a preliminary motion to determine whether the definition of "spouse" in the provincial legislation governing the insurance policy included common-law spouses. The motions court judge ruled that "spouse" referred to a legally married person, and the decision was affirmed by the Ontario Court of Appeal. M and V appealed to the Supreme Court of Canada on the issues of the definition of "spouse", and whether the definition infringed the equality rights guaranteed under s. 15 of the Canadian Charter of Rights and Freedoms.

A majority of the Supreme Court of Canada allowed the appeal. McLachlin J. spoke for four judges in holding that for the purposes of policy the word "spouse" applied to married persons only. On the issue of infringement of s. 15 of the Charter, the two-step approach to interpretation described by Cory J. in *Egan v. Canada (146)* was applied. The two-step approach afforded courts the opportunity to interpret s. 15 rights in a broad and generous fashion, leaving the task of narrowing the protection to conform to social and legislative interests to s. 1.

The first step was to show unequal treatment. The automobile insurance policy granted to married couples benefits which were denied to unmarried couples. The second step was to establish discrimination. Marital status was held to be an analogous ground under s. 15, touching the essential dignity and worth of the individual, such that there was discrimination. The legislation was found not to be justified under s. 1.

L'Heureux-Dubé J. assumed without deciding that "spouse" for the purposes of the policy referred only to a married person. She applied the same approach that she used in *Egan v. Canada (146)* to conclude that the legislation unjustifiably infringed s. 15 and to allow the appeal.

On behalf of four judges, Gonthier J. concluded that the word "spouse" was limited to married persons, but held that the limitation did not infringe s. 15 of the Charter. The mutual support obligations of married couples were different in essence from those of unmarried couples. Married couples choose to assume married status and accept the resultant support obligations defined by legislation. Such consensual mutual support obligations did not exist for nonmarried couples. The legislation in question was interpreted as being concerned with defining certain benefits whose functional value was to provide support for married couples. As a matter of social policy, there was no obligation on a legislature to extend all the attributes of marriage to unmarried couples.

148. *Thibaudeau v. Canada*
95 D.T.C. 5273 (S.C.C.)

The respondent, T, received from her former husband maintenance payments which were intended for the exclusive benefit of T's two children. T chose to report the payments as income on tax returns filed by her children. Revenue Canada reassessed T's return and on the basis of s. 56(1)(*b*) of the Income Tax Act included the maintenance payments in T's income. That section provided that any amount received by a taxpayer as a periodic allowance pursuant to a divorce decree was to be included in the taxpayer's income. Section 60(*b*) provided that such amounts paid out could be deducted in calculating the payor's taxable income. T appealed the assessment to the Tax Court of Canada, alleging that s. 56(1)(*b*)infringed her equality rights as guaranteed by s. 15 of the Canadian Charter of Rights and Freedoms. Her appeal was dismissed by the Tax Court but allowed by the Federal Court of Appeal.

A majority of the Supreme Court of Canada allowed the appeal. Gonthier J. observed that income of married parents, applied to the maintenance of their children, was taxed in the hands of the parents. Therefore, in the case of separated or divorced parents, it was necessary to look at the tax consequences for both parents. Sections 56(1)(*b*) and 60(*b*) of the Income Tax Act constituted an inclusion/deduction system for payments passing between divorced or separated individuals. If the marginal tax rate of the payor was greater than that of the recipient, the inclusion/deduction system resulted in a net benefit. If the marginal rate of the payor was less than that of the recipient, there was a net loss. If the marginal rates of the two parties were equal, there was neither a benefit or a loss.

Against that background, the answer to the constitutional issue involved the three-step process of determining whether or not there was a distinction, whether or not there was prejudice, and whether or not the distinction was based on an irrelevant personal characteristic. Gonthier J. found a distinction, but no prejudice. On the whole, separated or divorced parents received a net benefit from the inclusion/deduction system because most recipient parents had a lower marginal tax rate than that of the payors. Even with the distinction between recipient and payor, the total tax burden of the couple was reduced, allowing greater resources to be made available for the benefit of the children. The fact that the tax saving was not in equal proportion did not result in an infringement of s. 15. The trial judge who granted the divorce took into account the tax impact and found the amount of maintenance to be fair and equitable. Since there was no prejudice, there was no need to assess whether the distinction was based on an irrelevant personal characteristic.

Cory and Iacobucci JJ. saw this approach as depriving a s. 1 Charter analysis of its substantive role by importing into s. 15 the justificatory analysis properly belonging to s. 1. It focused on the grounds of discrimination, but failed to consider its impact. Under s. 15, the claimant bore the burden of proving the legislation to be discriminatory. Under s. 1, the government bore the onus of justifying any discrimination. In this case, there was no burden imposed by the Income Tax Act in the sense of denying a benefit. If there had been any disproportionate displacement of the tax liability, the responsibility for that fell on the family law system and not on the Income Tax Act.

In dissent, McLachlin J. held that by forcing one person to report as income an amount another person was allowed as a deduction, the tax scheme imposed a burden on custodial parents which it did not impose on noncustodial parents. The basis of distinction was status as a separated or divorced custodial parent. This was not enumerated in s. 15 but was found to be an analogous ground of discrimination. It was not justified under a proportionality test as there was no minimal impairment.

L'Heureux-Dubé J. also dissented, adopting the approach of focusing on the group adversely affected by the distinction and the nature of the interest affected to conclude that there was s. 15 infringement that could not be justified under s. 1.

149. *Symes v. Canada*
[1993] 4 S.C.R. 695, 110 D.L.R. (4th)

The appellant, S, was a lawyer and the mother of two children. She employed a nanny to take of her children. For four consecutive taxation years S deducted as a business expense the salary she paid to the nanny. The deductions were disallowed by Revenue Canada on the ground that the expenses were not outlays or expenses incurred for the purpose of gaining or producing income from business. The assessments for each of the four years were successfully challenged in the Federal Court, but the decision was reversed by the Federal Court of Appeal.

An appeal was taken to the Supreme Court of Canada on the issue of whether ss. 9, 18 and 63 of the Income Tax Act permitted deduction of child care expenses as a business expense and, if not, whether any of the sections infringed the equality rights guaranteed by s.15 of the Charter. Section 9 defined business income as profit. Section 18 prohibited taking deductions for business expenses incurred for purposes other than producing business income. Section 63 provided for a deduction to be taken in respect of child care expenses incurred to enable the taxpayer to work.

A majority of the Supreme Court of Canada dismissed the appeal. After an extensive analysis of the relevant provisions of the Income Tax Act, Iacobucci J. concluded that the Act did not permit a business expense deduction in respect of child care. In assessing whether there was infringement of s. 15, the sole focus of the argument was s. 63 of the Income Tax Act, which was found to be a complete code with respect to child care expenses. In order to show discrimination, S had to prove, not that women disproportionately bear the burden of child care in society, but that women disproportionately bear the cost of child care expenses. In the absence of such evidence, it was held that s. 63 did not create a distinction on the basis of sex.

In dissent, L'Heureux-Dubé J. agreed with much of the majority's analysis of the Income Tax Act and concluded that ss. 9 and 18 did not prohibit the deduction of child care costs as a business expense. Further, s. 63 did not override s. 9 and the two sections were not mutually inconsistent. However, on the assumption that the Income Tax Act did prohibit deduction of child care expenses, it would have infringed s. 15.

Language Rights

150. *Société des Acadiens du Nouveau-Brunswick Inc. v. Association of Parents for Fairness in Education, Grand Falls District 50 Branch*
[1986] 1 S.C.R. 549, 23 C.R.R. 119

The appellants sought injunctive and declaratory relief against a school board with respect to French immersion programs. After a decision was rendered a group of parents organized themselves into the Association of Parents for Fairness in Education. The respondent, A, sought leave to appeal the decision rendered in the dispute between the appellants and the school board. A hearing was scheduled before Stratton J.A. in the Court of Appeal, who was requested by the appellants to refer the matter to a bilingual judge. The judge complied with the request. The bilingual judge held that an application for leave to appeal by some-one not a party to the original action was a question of the inherent jurisdiction of the Court of Appeal and thus had to be decided by a panel of the Court. The panel that was appointed included Stratton J.A. The panel granted A leave to appeal.

The appellants brought the matter before the Supreme Court of Canada on the issue of whether s. 19(2) of the Canadian Charter of Rights and Freedoms entitled a party pleading in New Brunswick to be heard by a court whose members were capable of understanding all written and oral submissions regardless of the official language used by the parties.

A majority of the Supreme Court of Canada drew a parallel between the rights guaranteed by s. 19(2) of the Charter and s. 133 of the Constitution Act, 1867. The former provision permitted anyone to use either English or French in any proceedings in courts of New Brunswick. The latter permitted the use of either English or French in any proceedings of a court established under the Act. The rights granted were language rights unrelated to the requirements of natural justice. The rights vested in the speaker or writer or issuer of court processes. There was no guarantee in either of the provisions that the person in whom the rights vested would be understood, or would have a right to be understood, in the language of that person's choice.

The common-law right to be heard and understood by a court was not a language right but an aspect of the much broader right to a fair hearing. A party pleading in New Brunswick was held to be entitled to be heard by a court whose members understood both official languages, but this entitlement was derived from the principles of natural justice and from the Official Languages of New Brunswick Act, and not from s. 19(2) of the Charter.

Two other judges concluded that there was an entitlement to be heard, but that the entitlement was specifically derived from s. 19(2) of the Charter.

The Court was unanimous in finding that the appellants had not been denied a hearing or suffered a disadvantage as a result of the presence of Stratton J.A. on the panel. The appeal was dismissed.

151. *R. v. Mercure*
[1988] 1 S.C.R. 234, 48 D.L.R. (4th) 1

The appellant, M, was charged with speeding under the Vehicles Act of Saskatchewan and was issued a summons pursuant to the Summary Offences Procedure Act. He applied for permission to enter a plea in French and to have his trial conducted in French. No provincial statute provided for such an application.

Before Saskatchewan became a province it was subject to the North-West Territories Act. Section 110 of that Act provided for the use of English and French in proceedings before the Territorial Assembly and in the courts, and all ordinances were to be printed in both languages. Section 16 of the Saskatchewan Act provided that all laws applicable to the territory before the passage of the Act were to continue to apply to the province after the passage of the Act, subject to legislative repeal.

The trial judge interpreted these provisions as meaning that M was entitled to use French, but that the right could be satisfied by having an interpreter present in court. Also, there was no requirement on the Saskatchewan Legislature to print its enactments in both languages. The trial proceeded in English and M was convicted. His appeal was dismissed.

A further appeal was allowed and the conviction quashed by a majority of the Supreme Court of Canada. The legislation was clear that territorial provisions were to continue to apply to the province in the absence of repeal or inconsistency with the Saskatchewan Act. Section 110 was neither repealed nor was it inconsistent with the Act. This led to the conclusion that the unilingual Saskatchewan statutes were invalid as not having been enacted in the manner and form required by the Saskatchewan Act. However, the invalidity was resolved in the same manner as that in *Reference re Language Rights Under the Manitoba Act, 1870 (3)*, such that M's conviction could have been validly enforced.

M's request to have the trial conducted in French was denied on the basis of *Société des Acadiens du Nouveau-Brunswick Inc. v. Association of Parents for Fairness in Education (150)*. He was entitled to speak French, but had no right to require others to do so. However, he did have a right to enter a plea in French, which was denied. This denial vitiated the trial.

See also *Ford v. Quebec (Attorney General) (130)*

Minority Education Rights

152. *City of Winnipeg v. Barrett*
[1892] A.C. 445 (P.C.)

The Public Schools Act, 1890 declared itself to be applicable to all Protestant and Roman Catholic school districts in the Province of Manitoba. Under the Act all public schools were free schools and non-sectarian. Religious exercises were to be conducted according to the regulations of an advisory board, and were entirely at the option of the school trustees for the district. Any school not conducted according to the provisions of the Act was deemed not to be a public school and was not entitled to share in the portion of a legislative grant allotted to public schools. Prior to the passage of the Act there was a system of denominational education, with twelve school districts comprising mainly a Protestant population, and twelve school districts comprising mainly a Roman Catholic population.

Under the Manitoba Act, 1870, nothing in any provincial law was to prejudicially affect any right or privilege with respect to denominational schools which anyone had at the time of the Union with the Dominion. Pursuant to the Public Schools Act, the City of Winnipeg enacted by-laws authorizing assessments for school purposes. The by-laws were challenged on the ground that they prejudicially affected rights or privileges existing at the time of the Union. There were two appeals heard together. One was from a decision of the Supreme Court of Canada reversing a judgment upholding the validity of the by-laws. The other was from a decision of the Court of Queen's Bench following the decision of the Supreme Court of Canada.

On appeal, the Privy Council found that the denominational system was implemented by legislation after Manitoba had become a province. At the time of Union, there was not in force any law or regulation or ordinance with respect to education. Therefore, there were no rights or privileges existing by law with respect to denominational schools.

The respondents, B, contended that they could not send their children to public schools because the education would not have been supervised by church authorities. Therefore, they felt compelled to support their own schools but were still taxed for public schools, and this put them at a disadvantage as against those who could take advantage of the free public school system. The Privy Council acknowledged the argument, but held that the law was accessible to everyone. The Public Schools Act did not compel a child to attend a public school. Members of any religious body were free to establish and maintain and conduct schools anywhere in the province. The fact that the respondents could not partake of the provisions of the Act owing to religious convictions did not violate any right or privilege. The appeals were allowed.

153. *Ottawa Separate School Trustees v. Mackell*
[1917] A.C. 62 (P.C.)

The appellants, O, were elected trustees of the Roman Catholic separate schools established in Ottawa under the Separate Schools Act, 1863, which was legislation of the province of Upper Canada. The respondents, M, were supporters of those schools. The Common Schools Act, 1859, also legislation of Upper Canada, established common (public) schools for free primary education in the province. The Department of Education had power to make regulations for common and separate schools under both Acts. The Department made regulations affecting English-French schools, defined as those schools in which French was the primary language of instruction and communication. The courses of study in English-French schools were to be the same as those in public schools, French was preserved as a subject of study as long as it did not interfere with the adequacy of the

English instruction, and teachers required a knowledge of English sufficient to teach the prescribed courses of study.

The appellants did not comply with the regulations. The respondents brought an action for a mandatory order to conform to and enforce the regulations. The order was granted but the appellants failed to comply. A second order directed the appellants to open their schools in accordance with the law but they refused. The judgment was affirmed by the Court of Appeal.

On appeal to the Privy Council, it was held that the rights and privileges of the appellants were governed by the Common Schools Act. One section of that Act allowed the trustees to determine "the kind and description of schools to be established". The appellants argued that the "kind of school" meant a school where instruction in French was at least as important as instruction in English. The Privy Council rejected that argument, saying that "kind" referred to "character", as, for example, a girls' school, a boys' school or an infants' school. "Kind" did not relate to the language of instruction.

The regulation did not interfere with any rights vested in the French-speaking population, for there were no such rights vested by the British North America Act (the "BNA Act"). The only provision of the BNA Act relating to the use of English and French was directed to courts and legislatures, not to education or schools. The regulations were held to be *intra vires*, and the appeal was dismissed.

154. *Attorney General of Quebec v. Quebec Association of Protestant School Boards*
[1984] 2 S.C.R. 66, 9 C.R.R. 133

Section 72 of the Quebec Charter of the French Language ("Bill 101") provided that instruction in the kindergarten classes and elementary and secondary schools of Quebec was to be in French. Section 73 set out a list of exceptions to s. 72. Several motions were presented to the Superior Court to determine whether those sections were inconsistent with the Canadian Charter of Rights and Freedoms. The Superior Court found an inconsistency and held the provisions to be of no force and effect. Appeals to the Court of Appeal were dismissed.

The Supreme Court of Canada observed and the Crown acknowledged that Bill 101 and the Charter were incompatible in that the Charter granted certain minority language education rights which were limited under the provisions of Bill 101. However, the Crown argued that s. 1 of the Charter applied to guarantee the rights and freedoms conferred by s. 23, that s. 1 did not distinguish between the limit and denial of a right, and that the provisions of Bill 101 placed reasonable and demonstrably justifiable limits on s. 23 rights.

The Court accepted the first point as established without deciding it, but rejected the other two arguments. Section 23 of the Charter was an attempt to remedy the regime set out in Bill 101. The purpose of the framers of the section was "to adopt a general rule guaranteeing the Francophone and Anglophone minorities in Canada an important part of the rights which the Anglophone minority in Quebec had enjoyed with respect to the language of instruction" (at 84 S.C.R.) prior to the adoption of Bill 101. On that basis, the limits imposed by the Bill 101 regime could not possibly have been regarded by the framers of s. 23 as reasonable limits demonstrably justified under s. 1. Therefore, the provisions of Bill 101 were inconsistent with the Charter and of no force and effect.

155. *Mahe v. Alberta*
[1990] 1 S.C.R. 342, 46 C.R.R. 193

The appellants, M, brought an application under s. 23 of the Charter to create a French-language public elementary school in Edmonton. When their requests were not met they commenced an action seeking declarations stating that there were sufficient numbers of children in the metropolitan area of Edmonton to warrant provision of French language instruction from public funds under s. 23. The trial judge concluded that s. 23 bestowed a degree of exclusive management and control over the provision and administration of minority language schools, and that there was a sufficient number of students of French linguistic minority to warrant granting such rights, but did not grant the specific declarations sought. An appeal to the Alberta Court of Appeal was dismissed.

The Supreme Court of Canada defined the issues as whether s. 23 rights included a right to management and control of French language schools, and if so, whether there were sufficient numbers of students in the area to invoke the right. The proper interpretation of the section involved viewing it as providing a general right to minority language instruction with qualifications relating to instruction and facilities. These qualifications were not two separate rights; they defined the limits of a "sliding scale" of requirement, with "instruction" defining the lower limit and "facilities" defining the upper limit. This case involved a large number of s. 23 students and therefore was concerned with the upper limit.

It was held that s. 23(3)(*b*), which referred to facilities, mandated a measure of management and control where the numbers warranted. Such management and control was necessary because a variety of management issues in education could affect linguistic and cultural concerns. Such concerns were important because the general purpose of s. 23 was seen as preserving and promoting "the two official languages of Canada, and their respective cultures, by ensuring that each language flourishes . . . in provinces where it is not spoken by the majority of the population" (Whyte, Lederman & Bur, p. 27-24).

The measure of management and control depended on the number of students to be served. A large number might warrant an independent school board, whereas a lesser number might warrant linguistic minority representation on an existing school board. The number of students to be served was assessed on an estimate of the number of persons who would eventually take advantage of a proposed service. In this case, the level of demand for education in French was found to be sufficient to allow the minority language parents to be represented on the separate school board. The appeal was allowed.

Aboriginal Rights

156. *R. v. Sparrow*
[1990] 1 S.C.R. 1075, [1990] 4 W.W.R. 410

The appellant, S, was a member of the Musqueam Band. He was charged under s. 61(1) of the Fisheries Act with fishing with a drift net longer than that permitted by the terms of the band's food fishing licence. S contended that he was exercising an aboriginal right to fish and that the net length restriction was inconsistent with s. 35(1) of the Constitution Act, 1982, which recognized and affirmed existing aboriginal and treaty rights.

The trial judge held that there was no treaty, proclamation, contract or other document to support a claim to an aboriginal right. S was convicted and his appeal was dismissed by the County Court. The British Columbia Court of Appeal held that there was an aboriginal right to fish, but that they could not acquit on the facts as found by the trial judge. An appeal was taken to the Supreme Court of Canada on the issue of whether the net length restriction was inconsistent with s. 35(1) of the Constitution Act, 1982.

The Supreme Court held that the phrase "existing aboriginal rights" had to be interpreted flexibly to permit evolution, rather than defined according to the state of the law in existence in 1982. In this case, there was evidence that S had been fishing "in ancient tribal territory where his ancestors had fished from time immemorial" (Whyte, Lederman & Bur, p. 28-4). The Crown argued that the Fisheries Act and its regulations constituted a complete code inconsistent with the continued existence of an aboriginal right, but the Court held that nothing in the Act or regulations demonstrated a clear intention to extinguish the aboriginal right to fish. The scope of the right was held to be the right to fish for subsistence and for social and ceremonial purposes.

Each alleged infringement of s. 35(1) would have to be assessed on its own facts. In general, an inquiry would begin with a determination of whether the legislation in question interfered with an existing aboriginal right. That inquiry involved questions of whether there was an unreasonable limitation, an undue hardship, or a denial of a preferred means of exercising a right. Any interference found would have to be justified by establishing a valid legislative objective consistent with the

Crown's fiduciary relationship to aboriginals as set out in *Guerin v. the Queen (116)*. The Court suggested other possible factors in assessing justification, but did not purport to set out an exhaustive list.

Based on the findings of fact, which were insufficient to engage in a s. 35(1) analysis regarding the right to fish, a new trial was ordered to assess the constitutional question in light of the Supreme Court's analysis.

157. *Four B Manufacturing Ltd. v. United Garment Workers of America*
[1980] 1 S.C.R. 1031, 102 D.L.R. (3d) 385

The appellant, F, was incorporated under Ontario law. It operated a factory on the Bay of Quinte Band reserve pursuant to a permit issued under the Indian Act. The permit provided that the companywas to give employment preference to local people. Most of F's employees were members of the band, but some were former Band members and some were non-Indians. The respondent U was certified as bargaining agent for the production employees of F under the Ontario Labour Relations Act. F sought judicial review of the decision to certify U, on the ground that the labour relations of the company and its employees were not governed by provincial legislation. The decision was affirmed by the Divisional Court and the Court of Appeal.

A majority of the Supreme Court of Canada dismissed the appeal. Speaking for seven judges, Beetz J. observed that with respect to labour relations, provincial jurisdiction was the rule and federal jurisdiction the exception. F manufactured shoes, an operation which was not by its nature a federal undertaking.

F argued that the case concerned the civil rights of aboriginal people on a reserve, which was a matter for the exclusive legislative authority of Parliament. This argument was rejected as being an oversimplification. One of the issues involved the right of aboriginals and non-aboriginals alike to associate with one another for labour relations purposes. Another issue involved the relationship with the respondent U, which did not involve aboriginal rights. The employer F was privately owned by four brothers, all of whom were members of the band, but that was not seen to involve their civil rights. In this case neither Indian status nor rights necessarily incident to Indian status were at stake. Therefore, the power to regulate labour relations did not form an integral part of primary federal jurisdiction over aboriginal people and lands reserved for them.

F's alternate argument was that the Canadian Labour Code had occupied the field. However, the Code was directed to federal activities, operations or functions. It was not directed to individuals who might be considered "federal persons". It was already established that the operation of F was not a federal undertaking, therefore the majority rejected the argument.

The dissenting judges concluded that the operation in its direction and complement of employees was substantially an enterprise of Indians for Indians on an Indian reserve. It operated under a licence issued by the Minister of Indian Affairs and Northern Development. It therefore was an undertaking within the legislative authority of the Parliament of Canada such that certification to represent F's employees had to be sought under the Canada Labour Code.

INDEX